13 Animal Stories

Paul Groves
John Griffin
Nigel Grimshaw

Edward Arnold

© Paul Groves, John Griffin and Nigel Grimshaw 1984

First published in Great Britain 1984 by
Edward Arnold (Publishers) Ltd
41 Bedford Square, London WC1B 3DQ

Edward Arnold (Australia) Pty Ltd
80 Waverley Road, Caulfield East,
Victoria 3145, Australia

Reprinted 1987

British Library Cataloguing in Publication Data

Groves, Paul
    13 animal stories
    1. Children's stories, English
    2. Animals—Juvenile literature
    I. Title   II. Griffin, John, *1935–*
    III. Grimshaw, Nigel
    823′.01′0836[J]   PZ10.3

ISBN 0-7131-0957-2

Cover photography by courtesy of Stephen Dalton/NHPA.

Set in 12/14 Baskerville by ⅀ Tek-Art, Croydon, Surrey
Printed in Great Britain by Richard Clay Ltd, Bungay, Suffolk

Contents

To The Teacher

As in the other 13 books the aim in this book is to present a variety of stories. They range from the deeply serious to the light-hearted. Dealing with animals both wild and tame, some native to this country and some from abroad, these stories have a variety of approaches to the theme of animal life, and it is hoped that one of the attractions of the book will be the way in which it can open a perspective to children on how people and animals interdepend on this planet.

Each story is accompanied by questions which examine first the reader's depth of comprehension and go on to ask about wider implications of the material and the pupil's experience associated with it. There are questions on language use and suggestions for a variety of creative written work. As the questions range from the simple to the more demanding the book seems particularly suitable for mixed-ability classes.

Mercury

It was a moonlit night in 1942 during the Second World War. The pilot of the Wellington bomber looked desperately around for cloud cover. Soon he would cross the Danish coast. The German guns would see him and hell would leave its dark caverns of the earth and live in the dark caverns of the night sky.

He was on an important mission. On board was not the normal bomb load but canisters containing one hundred pigeons from the top pigeon breeders of Britain. The pigeons were to be parachuted to the Danish Resistance, loyal Danes who fought at great risk for the freedom of their homeland from Nazi rule. Each pigeon that reached them would be sent back to Britain. In a special capsule on its leg would be a message from them. The British were desperate to know about the exact positions of certain German weapons and military targets.

Suddenly the searchlights criss-crossed in front of the Wellington, the tell-tale white puffs of exploding shells appeared in front of the pilot and the plane began to rock.

He swung the plane this way and that and then happily the moonlight disappeared and the plane had the sanctuary of cloud cover. A few more miles and the dropping zone agreed with the Resistance would be reached.

The pilot came in as low as he dared for accuracy and dropped his winged load. In canister No. 3, Mercury, a pigeon belonging to Mr Jim Catchpole of Ipswich, felt that sensation she had felt several times before on other missions. She was dropping but in no way could she control the drop with her wings. Desperately she tried to beat them but there was no room in the small basket. This short drop seemed a long agony to her until there was a bone-shaking bump. Then she was tipped over on her side and she couldn't regain her feet. Her wings beat against the basket but to no avail. She was in complete darkness as she had been for several hours.

Suddenly the fierce light of a torch flared into her eyes. Her body stiffened. She was relieved to find a gentle hand cradling her from the basket. At once her confidence returned in the warmth of the cupped hands. It was not her owner; her owner's hands were gentler and a touch of panic went through her body.

Water was placed in front of her but she had no great thirst. She pecked listlessly at the bowl. Then something was attached to her leg and she was thrown up into the semi-darkness.

The sun was just rising. She circled once to get her bearings. She heard the comforting beat of other wings but could not pick out any of her companions. Then something in her brain locked into the direction of Ipswich in England and she set off into the moist dawn.

As the sun rose gradually she reached the Danish coast. To her left were two other pigeons flying slightly lower. To her right were three more. The sun's rays reflected on their under feathers.

Suddenly there was a crack and one of the pigeons to her left seemed to stop in the air, twist and fall in a gyrating spiral. There were more cracks. Below the German soldiers had spotted the six pigeons and were trying to shoot them all. Mercury sensed the danger and flew higher, changing her direction slightly from time to time but still swept on towards Ipswich. That was some four hundred and eighty miles away. The sea to be crossed was the North Sea — a cold stretch of water — where the wind was blowing from the west against her.

More cracks and another pigeon spiralled down. But Mercury was now out of range. She dipped down again and flew just a few metres over the sea. The four pigeons were now in close formation. But suddenly they were in a patch of sea mist. Mercury felt disorientated; her brain played her tricks. She was not sure that she was going in the right direction. But her instinct and a dogged determination kept her going towards the English coast. When the mist cleared, only three pigeons flew out of it.

Half-way across the North Sea was reached with no more trouble. Occasionally they would see a small fishing boat or naval vessel. The masts looked inviting but Mercury knew that if she once stopped she was finished.

Now the wind rose against them in strength. It whistled across their ears and eyes. One pigeon suddenly peeled away and plunged into the sea.

The two remaining birds sensed that the wind would be less strong if they flew just above the waves. They flew in this way for more than fifty miles. Then everything went grey as a huge wave smashed over them. Mercury just caught the top spray. The other pigeon was drowned. Mercury was now on her own. She had many miles to go.

The wind dropped but the sun became hot. She was desperate for water. Her wings felt as if they were peeling from her body. Would she see her loft again?

She now flew mechanically. She had to dig into her reserves to keep the wings going. It was sheer instinct that kept her above the waves. She kept going straight. She felt any turn to right or left would send her down.

Then at last there was the coastline. She could see the foam breaking on the beach. But the loft was still twenty miles away and in her condition electric cables were a great danger.

At last the black and white of her loft roof came into view. She swooped down with the dregs of her energy.

Her owner, Mr Jim Catchpole, had been gazing anxiously into the sky with binoculars for three hours. He jumped when he saw her. 'Good girl!' he cried.

She landed and went into her loft to the welcome water and food. But first the important message had to be taken from her leg. Mr Catchpole gave her a cuddle and kissed her back as he took it off. He then hurried round on his bike to the local police station.

Of the one hundred pigeons sent the night before only Mercury got back. The message she carried was so important that it has never been revealed. She was awarded the Dickins' Medal, the animal V.C., one of thirty-nine pigeons to be honoured in the Second World War. She lived another five years and her descendants are still flying today.

Think It Over

1 Where was the bomber going?
2 What was on board instead of bombs?
3 Who were the pigeons sent to?
4 What made the white puffs?
5 Why was the pilot glad when the moon disappeared?
6 What was frightening to the pigeon in the drop?
7 Where was the pigeon flying back to?
8 What were the German soldiers trying to do?
9 Which way was the wind blowing? Why was this bad?
10 What causes Mercury to become confused?
11 What happens to each of the six pigeons?
12 Was the message she carried ever known?

Do You Know?

1 Who was Mercury in the Roman stories?
2 Name two other Second World War British bombers.
3 In which direction from you is the North Sea?

4 What country is Denmark joined to?
5 Name another country that had resistance fighters in the Second World War.
6 The guns that fired the shells were also known as a . . . a . . . guns.
7 Why did the sun's rays reflect on the under feathers?
8 What does V.C. stand for?

Using Words

1 What words would you use to describe a moonlit sky?
2 Which of these words means the same as 'mission': task; chore; assignment; job; duty; quest?
3 'listlessly' Give another word meaning this.
4 'Ipswich' Which towns in Britain are spelt with a capital letter?
5 What is the word in the story meaning: not knowing the way you are going?
6 'foam breaking on the beach' This can also be called . . . horses.
7 'binoculars' What does 'bi' attached to the front of a word mean?

Write Now

1 Write a story about any animal that helps people from the point of view of the animal.
2 You are in the Danish resistance with someone else. You wait for the pigeons. You see the moon. You hear gunfire. What do you talk about as you wait? Write a few lines as a play.
3 You are a bird or in an aeroplane. You fly above your home area. What do you see? Make a list.
4 Find out these facts about racing pigeons:
   a) How do they race?
   b) What kind of distances do they race?
   c) How are they trained?
Now write a short story or a poem called 'Racing Pigeon'.

Guilt

In the days before combine harvesters there were cart-horses. They were huge animals with great sturdy legs, long lashing tails and backs so broad that you had to do the splits to ride on them. Bill Judson was ten, old enough to work from seven in the morning until nine at night in those days. Bill's first job in the morning was to catch and harness the cart-horses. There were four on his dad's farm: Paddy, Captain, a fierce chestnut called Jean and an old white one known as Brothy's horse. Brothy was an old man who owned two small fields. When he decided to plough them up he had nowhere to put his horse, so he lent it to Bill's dad until he sold it.

At seven o'clock Bill made his way through the still damp grass to the big sycamore tree where the four huge horses lay. They turned their heads and looked at him suspiciously. They couldn't see the bridle he held behind his back but they knew he had come to catch them for a hard day's work pulling carts laden with sheaves of corn for stacking in the farm buildings. They stirred uneasily and Jean began to climb to her feet. Bill took a handful of the juiciest damp grass and held it towards her; if he could catch her the others would follow her to the stables for saddling.

Gently does it. Jean began to munch the grass from Bill's left hand as he brought his right hand holding the bridle from behind his back. If he could get the bit safely between her munching jaws then — but she snorted at the sight of the bridle, snatched the last of the grass, arched back her head and lumbered fifty metres to the edge of the paddock. Paddy and Captain followed her. Brothy's horse, more docile, was still lying on the grass.

'I suppose I'd better start with you,' said Bill, and was soon leading the huge white animal towards the stables. Its joints creaked from its long lie in the wet grass.

It was half an hour before all the horses were caught, saddled and placed in their carts. Bill's job was to lead the full carts from the field and return with the empty ones after the sheaves had been unloaded and stacked. It was tricky work, manoeuvering the carts through narrow gates, especially when it was Jean's turn. About midday she lurched to the left just as the cart wheels were coming through the gate. One caught the gatepost and some of the load of sheaves slipped to the ground. Bill cursed Jean and carried on to the stackyard.

'What you got there?' shouted the man whose job was to pass the sheaves to the stacker.

'Half of it's against yon gatepost,' shouted Bill.

'Who loaded it?'

'Bob Lord, I reckon. But it wasn't his fault. It's this damned horse. It won't go straight.'

'When I was an old boy, I got my backside warmed with a fork if I lost a load,' said the man.

Bill said nothing. The men always said that leading horses was an 'old boy's job', by which they meant 'easy', but he'd like to see them try, especially with Jean. He led Brothy's horse with its empty cart back to the field, stopping on the way to load the sheaves that had fallen near the gatepost. This made him late.

'Thought you'd knocked off. Where you been?'

'Lost a few sheaves and had to pick them up.'

'A few. Damn near half a load. We don't go loading 'em for you to shake them off.'

By seven o'clock Bill was hungry, dirty and exhausted. There had been two more spillages and more insults.

'Come on, old lad; this'll be the last one for you,' he

said as he took Brothy's horse to the field. 'You've been the best one all day. Twenty times as good as that Jean.'

'Shall I come back again?' Bill asked his dad, as he took Captain's bridle to take the full load back.

'Yes, we can get a couple more loads in before it's too damp.' This didn't please the men, especially Bob Lord, who was loading.

'The dew's coming up pretty fast. The last few sheaves were real damp. We ought to knock off after this one.'

'All right, but make it a good 'un,' Bill's dad agreed.

So half an hour later the biggest load of the day set off in the gathering dusk pulled by the oldest horse. But Brothy's horse was willing, if weakening. The ground sloped up just before the last gate. There the ruts were deepest and the wheels ground to a halt.

'Get up,' said Bill's dad, giving Brothy's horse a tap on its rear with his hay-fork.

The old horse strained and wheezed, the men leant their weight to the wheels and gradually the cart moved the last few metres to the haystack.

Bill was waiting for it. While the men put tarpaulins over the stack and the last load, Bill undid the linking chains and led Brothy's horse to the stable. When he'd taken off the bridle, saddle and collar there were great dark sweat patches showing up against its white coat.

'Off you go, old chap. You did well,' said Bill and patted it on the head. It trotted out of the stable towards the field. It took Bill a quarter of an hour to hang up the horses' tackle ready for the morning. Then he shut the stable door and went to the barn.

The first thing he saw was Brothy's horse with its head in the corn bin, munching the chickens' wheat.

'Get up!' he shouted desperately and pulled its head away. It backed off and lumbered slowly to the field.

'Hey Dad,' he shouted. 'Brothy's horse has been at the wheat.'

'Damn. Who left the barn door open?'

'I reckon I did,' said Bill sadly.

'How much has it had?' said his dad angrily.

'I don't know. I let it out about five minutes ago,' lied Bill.

'Maybe it'll be all right then. Go and try to catch it before it gets to the pond.'

It was dusk now but he could pick out the huge white horse with its head down drinking great draughts of the still, greeny water. Bill ran to the pond.

'Get up, you stupid horse,' he gasped, pulling at its head. 'You'll die, you great stupid thing. The water'll swell the wheat and burst you.'

But no matter how hard he tugged, the horse wouldn't budge until it had drunk its fill.

'I couldn't stop it,' he told his dad.

'Well, maybe it'll be all right. Depends how much wheat it's had.'

'Shouldn't we get the vet?'

'What, this time of night? No, let's go and have a drink.'

Just before Bill went to bed he slipped down to the paddock. All four horses were standing under the sycamore tree, three huge dark shapes and one white one, picked out clearly by the moon. The horses stirred but didn't move away; they knew Bill hadn't come to catch them at that time of night. Bill went up to Brothy's horse. It was standing stock-still. It lifted its head slowly away. Was it Bill's imagination that made him think it was breathing more heavily than usual?

'I'm sorry, boy,' said Bill and trailed slowly home through the now damp grass.

When Bill woke it was still dark; he sat up in bed. Then he remembered Brothy's horse. He peered from his window towards the sycamore tree. The moon was even brighter. He could easily see the dark shapes of the horses. Three were still standing but one was a shapeless bundle on the ground.

'What's up?' said Bill's dad, sleepily.

'Brothy's horse is down.'

'It'll be resting. Anyway, there's nothing we can do now.'

Before Bill had finished dressing, his dad was snoring again. The first streaks of day were showing in the East as he picked his way through the soaking grass. He could hear Brothy's horse gasping and wheezing from thirty metres away. It was lying on its side, its neck stretched out and its eyes dilated and unseeing. Bill knelt down and stroked its head. The other three horses stirred uneasily.

'I'm sorry,' said Bill and tears of shame and sadness started to form in his eyes. Brothy's horse was breathing in great rattling gasps with long pauses in between. Bill stroked his forehead for five minutes. Then he could stand the noise no longer.

The horse's swollen stomach reminded him of the time his dad had called the vet to a cow that had blown itself up by eating something it shouldn't. The vet had brought out a long, sharp, steel rod and driven it hard into the cow's belly. There was a hissing noise like escaping gas and gradully the swollen belly had returned to normal. Bill ran to the barn and looked desperately for something sharp. He picked up a broken hay-fork; it had one rusty prong left. Back he went to the sycamore tree. Brothy's horse hadn't moved and its breathing was unchanged. Bill pressed the fork against its stomach, but the rusty prong made no impression on the skin. Bill knew deep down that he was only pretending to do something. He didn't know where to press and in any case he was sure it wasn't the same problem as the cow's.

The gasps now came more slowly and at each one the

whole body of Brothy's horse shuddered.

'Die! Why don't you die!' muttered Bill. Then suddenly he could stand the choking noise no longer. Bill ran to the house and down the cellar steps. He could just see his dad's twelve-bore shotgun in the grey light. Bill was going to shoot Brothy's horse. He rummaged in the drawer for a couple of live cartridges. He knew the pellets spread wide. He'd have to put the gun right to the horse's head, if he could. Would it really kill it or only tear a piece from its neck? Bill walked back slowly, torn with indecision. When he reached the sycamore tree he could hear only the breathing of the other horses. Brothy's horse was dead.

Bill put down the gun and knelt by its side. There's something terrible about the death of a big animal, especially if you've been responsible for it. Only a few hours ago it was pulling a heavy cart full of sheaves. It didn't seem possible it would never stand up again. Its eyes were wide and staring and its teeth bared. Bill stroked its neck; already it was beginning to go cold. Bill wondered what it was like to die. He imagined that you would just see the kind of red you get when you shut your eyes tightly. Did it hear him or was his talk just tiny noises that were happening miles away?

Bill went back to bed. He lay on his back thinking about Brothy's horse and how he'd really murdered it. He listened to his dad's snoring. He turned his pillow several times. Soon the pillow was wet on both sides.

The next thing Bill knew he was woken by voices in the yard outside his house. The sun was high in the sky. He went to his window. Old Brothy, white-whiskered and bald-headed was talking to Bill's dad. They were looking towards the sycamore tree. Brothy's horse was moving. It was sliding slowly along the ground being pulled by a chain round its neck. Gradually the huge white body was winched up the boards onto the trailer. Soon the trailer sides were slammed to and the knacker's lorry turned and drove out of the gate. The last Bill saw of the horse was its head hanging dead over the side of the trailer.

'It was getting on,' Bill heard his dad say to Brothy.

'Ah, maybe it was. But it were still a shock. I mean there was nowt up with it last week.'

'I'm sorry,' said Bill's dad. 'I'm as surprised as you.'

'Maybe you worked it too hard,' said the old man.

'No chance of that,' said Bill's dad. 'You can ask Bob Lord or the others. It was just pulling wagons, as normal.'

'Maybe it were summat it 'ad etten,' said Brothy, sadly.

'Nothing as I know of,' said Bill's dad.

Bill dressed and went downstairs. He joined his dad and watched Brothy walking sadly down the drive.

'Why didn't you tell him?' said Bill.

'What good would that do? Only upset him.'

'It's not right,' said Bill, beginning to cry again.

'There's a lot of things not right,' said Bill's dad. 'But it's no use getting yourself upset about them.'

'It was my fault,' sobbed Bill.

'Come and get yourself some breakfast,' said his dad.

Think it Over

1 What was Bill's first job in the morning?
2 What was Jean known as?
3 Why does Bill want to catch Jean first?
4 Which horse does Bill catch first?
5 What was Bill's job?
6 Why are the men in the field annoyed?
7 What time of the day did the last load go in?
8 What mistake does Bill make? Who else might be to blame?
9 What did Bill try to do for the sick horse?
10 How does Bill feel about the death of the horse?
11 Where was the dead horse taken?

Do You Know?

1　How was the harvest collected in the days of the story?
2　What is a cornrick? What is a sheaf?
3　What does a combine harvester do?
4　What was the name of the craftsmen who made and re-paired cart wheels?
5　What kind of 'fork' is referred to?
6　Why does corn need to be collected in a dry state?
7　Why should a horse not eat wheat then drink?
8　Should Bill's dad have told the truth? Why didn't he?

Using Words

1　'lumbered' Can you think of any other words that might describe a cart-horse at work? What words would you use for a tractor?
2　What does 'docile' mean? What animal would not be docile?
3　How do you write dialect words to show letters not pro-nounced?
4　'tackle' Give two meanings for this word in sentences of your own.
5　'draughts' Give three meanings for this word in sen-tences of your own.

Write Now

1　In a few sentences describe how you feel when you are out of breath.
2　Write a short scene as a play about being late and making excuses for it.
3　Write about when you felt guilty of having caused harm to a living creature.
4　Describe a field of corn on a windy summer's day. It could be a short unrhymed poem.

The Chase

Rann came out of his hiding place where he had been resting after his night's hunting and stretched his back. Something had disturbed him and he sniffed the air.

He was a four-year-old dog fox. Reddish-brown on his back and white below, he was slightly bigger than most foxes. His ears, tipped with darker brown, twitched.

It was a grey day and there was very little breeze. Rann licked his nose to improve his sense of smell. He tilted his head slightly back and moved it from side to side, examining the wide range of scents that came to him. What breeze there was, was cold. That day the air was cooler than the ground and there was a tinge of winter in it.

Suddenly he stiffened. One scent out of the many that came to him was more frightening than the starvation and cold of winter could ever be. He was as still as stone, listening and concentrating on that scent of danger.

On the grass that stretched away in front of Hartoft Hall there were horses and their riders and a pack of hounds. Servants were passing through the crowd with trays of sherry. The riders, black-capped and black or red-coated, bent from their saddles to take a glass. There was a babble of conversation going on.

'Morning, Jeremy.'

'Morning, Gavin. Is the wife here?'

'No. Corfu for a week.'

'Hello, Fiona. You do look super.'

'Oh, I say. Thanks.'

The huntsman, Jack Wiggins, saluted the Master, a

Colonel Lennox-Temple.

'Going to be a good day, Wiggins,' the Master said.

'Looks like it, sir.'

'We'll draw Hangman's Covert, eh?'

'Right, sir. When you're ready.' Wiggins, a thin man with cold blue eyes in a narrow face, moved away.

From the Hangman's Covert, a stretch of woodland over a mile away, Rann could pick out the faint sounds and, from time to time, even detect a flicker of scent — the stink of horses, the sharp smell of hounds and of man. Then the sounds changed and the scents eddied and he knew they were on the move.

Wiggins started the hounds at the other end of the woods. They moved about quickly, seeking scent. The rest of the hunt were still chatting, their horses stirring restlessly. Rann had come home that way, though, after his night's hunting. Tranter, the leading hound, picked up his trail and gave tongue. Then the rest of the pack joined in, yelping, baying and jostling together and things began to move in a rush.

Rann fled down the well-known track and out of the wood at that first sound. He did not judge or plan in a human way but he could work out how far behind him the pack was and he knew what tricks might save his life.

He was out of the wood, running at full stretch, and over the wall at the end of it before the hunt caught sight of him. Ahead were fields of winter grass. To his left was another field, almost bare and brown, where a crop had been harvested. Scent was harder to follow on cleared soil. He veered left, crossed that field, another, yet another beyond that and streaked downhill to the road. He paused, crouched low by the hedge and heard the hounds casting about for his trail above him.

They were having difficulty in tracing him across the broken earth of that first field. The hunt had checked as

15

the hounds raced about crossing and re-crossing it. The Master rode up to Wiggins.

'Over the hill, Wiggins.' He pointed to the crest of the downland up to the right. 'That's where he'll have gone.'

'I don't think so, sir.' Wiggins knew the downland. It was a place where a hunted animal would leave a clear trail. He thought this fox would know that, too.

'He'll be off down there.' He indicated the road and began to ride towards it.

When the cry of hounds broke out once more, Rann began to trot along the road. It took him at right angles to the pursuit and not away from it, but he had made no mistake. Lower down the road, the hedge bordering it changed to stone walls.

Rann leapt from the road to the top of the wall, ran along it for twenty metres or so and then jumped down into the road again. He did the same thing on the other wall before he made for a clump of birch trees about a mile further on. There he stopped and rested again.

He had to guard against two things. Over a long run the hounds would be faster than he was. If they could keep him running to the pitch of exhaustion, he would be caught. Besides that, he had to stay on ground he knew. If he was driven off it into unknown country, his chances of survival would be small.

He was sweating, as dogs and foxes do, through his tongue and he was breathing quickly but he had plenty of strength left. The boundary of well-known territory was not far ahead of him. When he next moved, he would have to veer right or left. He could hear the hunt questing about for his trail.

'Lost him, Wiggins?' the Master was demanding.

'Not yet, sir.'

'Crafty devil, this one, eh?'

'We'll run him down, sir,' Wiggins said.

Almost as he spoke, the hounds found scent and the

16

hunt surged forwards.

They were hot on Rann's track then for what seemed hours. Once he held them back by running through a flock of sheep. Once he got another breathing space by going through a farm. A dog jumped out on him there and chased him for a few metres. That, too, had spoiled his scent and he had been able to recover some of his strength by trotting along slowly afterwards, hearing the hunt noise grow fainter behind him. Rann knew nothing of Wiggins, who was as dogged and wily as he was but each time the huntsman had found his fox again.

Now the pack was close behind Rann, slowly drawing nearer. He knew the fear of death: but he had one last hope.

Almost at the edge of that stretch of country he knew so well was a stream. Late in the afternoon, he came down to it. He was thirsty but dared only lap at the water for a second. In three leaps he crossed the stream and then ran up it on the other side, splashing through the shallower water by the bank. He could hear the hunt coming blood-chillingly loudly down the hill but he kept on in the water, crossing and re-crossing from bank to bank and glad of the shelter of the trees that overhung the stream. He had covered over a hundred metres before he turned and darted up the opposite hillside.

At the top he slumped down in the shelter of a clump of brambles. In front of him the sun was low and red in the darkening sky. His breath rasped burningly in his chest and his tired legs ached and trembled. Had he lost them at last? As his breathing grew easier, his eyelids flickered and he half-dozed.

He sprang up with a start. They were after him again. He realised that he was leaving country that he knew and ran wildly at first this way and that. He wanted to circle round the hunt so that he could double back to home ground. Then he saw it was useless. He glimpsed them on the hillside below, spread out in a long line, cutting off all hope of escape. They saw him, too. The hounds put on speed and the riders urged their tired horses forward. He fled away into unknown territory.

He had not got far, however, before he swerved. Before him ran something frightening which was not a stream or road or track. Had he been here before? A memory stirred faintly in his tired brain. For a while he ran alongside the strange barrier, seeking a safe way across while the hunt drew rapidly nearer.

Then the dim memory became clearer. The railway line might be terrifying because of the stink of the roaring monsters that had moved along it but it also offered hope. Gathering all his courage, he jumped up on one of the rails and ran delicately along it, balancing like a tight-rope walker.

He sensed that the steel would not hold his scent. If he could run far enough along the rail, keeping out of sight, he could still lose his enemies. But the hounds spotted him. They were racing forward up the brow of the hill. Rann leapt sideways off the rail and leapt again over the stones of the track. Forgetting his tiredness, he went like the wind into the brushwood on the other side.

But he had neither seen nor heard the hunt. What had sent him into cover was the drumming of the steel rail under his balancing feet. It thrilled through all his limbs as he felt the oncoming thunder of the train.

Wiggins had heard it, too, and was galloping madly to the top of the hill, yelling to his whipper-in. The two of them managed to hold back the hounds and to drive them away from the track as the long train rushed through. Scared by the wind and roar of its engine and its coaches, some of the hounds ran back downhill and some riders had trouble with their jumpy horses.

It took time for the train to pass and for things to get

18

sorted out. In the gathering dusk, the Master rode up to Wiggins.

'I'll set 'em on again, sir,' Wiggins suggested eagerly.

'No. It's getting late. It's been a good run,' the Master said. 'We'll have him another time.'

'We will that, sir,' Wiggins agreed grimly.

Rann was nearly a mile away. When all signs and sound of the hunt had disappeared, he returned to his home ground. If he had understood Wiggins' threat, he would not have cared. Animals have short memories and no idea of the future. By the next morning Rann had re-covered from his run. Well-fed, he was asleep in one of his lairs in Hangman's Covert. With the warm, red brush of his tail wrapped round him, he was dreaming of a land without winter, where there was plenty of food and where hounds, horses and man were never seen.

Think It Over

1   How old was Rann?
2   Where did the hunt meet?
3   Where did they start to hunt?
4   Which hound first picked up Rann's scent?
5   When he began to run, why did Rann choose to go across a cleared field rather than grass?
6   Why did Rann run along the walls by the lane?
7   Why did Rann have to avoid unknown country?
8   How did it help Rann to have the farm dog chase him?
9   Why did he spend so much time crossing and re-crossing the stream?
10   In what way might the sight of the sinking sun have given him hope?
11   What stopped him from circling back to home ground?
12   How might the steel railway line have saved him?
13   How did the coming of the train save him?
14   How did Rann feel the next morning about the hunt?

Do You Know?

1 What had disturbed Rann at the beginning of the story?
2 Which scent was most frightening to him?
3 Who knows more about foxes, Mr Wiggins or the Master? Give some evidence for your answer.
4 Name two ways in which Rann disguised his scent.
5 What other animals are hunted in this country?
6 What sort of food do foxes eat?

Using Words

1 What sort of a fox is a 'vixen'?
2 'a flock of sheep' What single word describes a group of: cows; hounds; bees; teachers working in a school?
3 'Tranter ... gave tongue' You could also say that Tranter 'bayed', a sound between a howl and a growl. What single word describes the sound made by each of the following animals: a cat; a donkey; a mouse; an elephant; a bee?
4 'To his left was another field ... *where a crop had been harvested*.' Add a sentence of your own to each of the following to make one longer sentence.
   a) ... where a fire had been lit.
   b) ... where his car was parked.
   c) ... where you found the purse.
   d) ... where red paint had been splashed.

Write Now

1 List five things — which could include food — which have the most pleasant smells you can think of.
2 Write a story about a person who is chased. It could be someone of your own age being chased by other children; it could be a criminal on the run, or it could be an escaped prisoner-of-war. You might have other ideas. Is the person caught in the end or does he or she get away?
3 Describe what you feel about hunting as a sport.

20

The Savage Bull

The three boys raced across the road to the five-barred gate. Ian threw the cricket bat over, Mark a stump and the ball, and John the remaining two stumps. Then they started to climb the gate frantically; the first one to have both feet in the field would have first innings. Ian won, John was second and Mark, who'd tried to hurdle the gate, fell back winded on the wrong side.

'I bat, John bowls and you're wicket-keeper,' said Ian unsympathetically to the fallen hurdler.

'Look at this,' said Mark, pointing to the gate.

'Look at what?' said John.

'Beware of the Bull, it says.'

'Liar. You're just trying to get us back over there so you can jump over first.'

But Mark was right. The message was in big chalk capitals. The three looked round the field they'd played cricket in illegally for the past fortnight. There were large hedges, a few trees at the far end near the pond, but no sign of a bull.

'Mr Tinkler's just trying to scare us off,' said Ian.

Mr Tinkler had turned them out twice in the last week. The last time he'd threatened to tell the local policeman. They decided that he was now trying to scare them with an imaginary bull, so they set up the stumps, started to play and forgot about the bull. Then John bowled a fast wide, Ian missed and the ball rolled away to the far end of the field. Mark trudged after it. Just before he reached the ball he turned and ran towards the gate as if he was doing the hundred metres in the Olympics. The other two stared in amazement at him, but then ran as fast as he when the huge black bull emerged from behind the trees near the pond. When they were safely over the gate they looked back at the bull. It was enormous. Its head was pointing in their direction, its ears were cocked and its long tail was swishing. The yellow ring in its nose glinted in the sunlight. Then the bull lowered its head.

'It's going to charge,' said Ian. 'Let's get going.'

But instead of charging, the bull lifted its head and began to chew.

'It's eating the ball,' said John. He turned to Mark angrily. 'Why didn't you bring the ball?'

'Why didn't you bring the stumps and the bat?' said Mark.

The three boys watched miserably as the huge animal chewed away at their new cricket ball.

'Excuse me,' said a girl's voice behind them. They turned to see a smart-looking girl of about eighteen, wearing a blue skirt and a white blouse and carrying a bucket in each hand. The boys moved aside and watched in amazement as she unlatched the gate, and walked calmly towards the bull. It lumbered towards her, head down. When girl and·bull met, she emptied the buckets in front of it. The bull spat out the last of the cricket ball and tucked into its feed. The girl patted it on the nose and returned with the empty buckets. She calmly undid the gate, shut it behind her and was about to walk to the blue car she'd parked on the other side of the road.

'Excuse me,' said John.

'What?' said the girl looking scornfully at the three grubby boys.

'Is that your bull?'

'Yes.'

'What's its name?'

'Morris.'

'Is it fierce?'

22

'Very.'

'It didn't seem fierce to you.'

'That's because it knows me. If you went anywhere near it, it would spin you round on its horns like a catherine wheel.'

'What's it doing in Mr Tinkler's field?' asked Mark.

'It's resting before it goes back to Spain for the bullfighting season.'

'You're having us on,' sneered Ian.

'Oh, am I, little boy? – Morris killed three bullfighters last season. If you want to try your luck, go ahead. He'd eat you for his breakfast.'

The girl turned scornfully away. She was just about to get into the car when Ian said desperately.

'Please would you get our bat and stumps?'

The girl looked across the field and laughed.

'Get them yourself, if you dare. It serves you right for trespassing.'

Then she was in the car and away. The boys watched her go. They looked at Morris eating his cattle cake.

They all agreed the girl was lying, but none of them was sure enough to dare venture into the field. They walked sadly home.

'You know that girl's blue skirt and white blouse,' said John.

'What about 'em?'

'My sister's got a skirt and blouse like that. And what's more that girl's hair was short and blond — like Ian's. Now if Ian went in that field dressed in Jane's skirt and blouse carrying a bucket, that bull wouldn't know the difference between him and . . .'

'No way,' said Ian.

But the bat was new and the stumps borrowed from Ian's uncle, who hadn't been keen to lend them in the first place, so it wasn't too surprising that at eleven o'clock the next morning Ian was hiding behind a bush

with his trousers and shirt stuffed in a bucket. He was
waiting for John to give the signal that no cars were coming and it was safe for a boy wearing a white blouse and
a blue skirt to cross the road and try to fool Morris.

Morris was fooled. He strode from his shady tree when
he thought he saw the girl with the bucket. Ian veered
carefully away from him towards the bat and stumps. He
caught sight of Morris's huge muscular legs and shoulders and shivered a little underneath his blouse. Suddenly Ian dropped the bucket, grabbed the bat and
stumps, seized the bucket handle again and belted for
the gate. Morris stared at him with his little pink eyes,
wondering whether to charge. Ian was cheered by his
friends as bucket, stumps, bat and boy dressed as girl fell
in a heap on the safe side of the gate.

'At least nobody saw me,' said Ian triumphantly.

But there he was wrong. That night Ian's dad said:

'That nosy old Ethel Turner's going funny in the head.
She told me she'd seen Ian dressed in a skirt and blouse
running across the Low Road near Casthorpe.'

'Where was she?' said Ian going red.

'You don't mean to say it's true?'

'No, course not,' muttered Ian, going redder.

They played cricket on the village green for two days,
but it wasn't as good. There were too many dogs and
small children in the way. Besides, the thought of Morris
haunted them. Had he really killed three bullfighters?
How did he charge? Were there any battle scars on him?

They walked towards Morris very slowly, their hearts
beating and their legs shaking but ready to run. Morris
stared at them, not bothering to move away from his
shady tree. He couldn't see a bucket, so he hadn't much
hope of food.

'Hello Morris,' said John.

Morris lowered his head slowly, his huge horns curved

and sharp. But he didn't charge. They inched forward. Mark took a carrot from his pocket and held it at arm's length. Morris's nose came forward; his large shiny nostrils dilated; he sniffed the carrot; he liked the smell. Out came a huge rough pink tongue; the whole carrot and stalk disappeared. Morris chewed contentedly.

'He's as tame as a hamster,' said Ian.

And so he was. He ate fifteen carrots, and lumbered slowly after them when they went for more. In the afternoon they played bucking broncos, each taking it in turn to lower himself on Morris's huge back from a branch of the tree. The only trouble was Morris wouldn't buck. Mark had a stop-watch to see how long John could stay on. After twenty minutes he pulled him off Morris to have a go himself. Morris eventually stooped his head to chew some grass. Mark slid onto his horns, Morris turned his head and deposited him on the floor, but showed no signs of annoyance. Two days later they became bored by Morris's lack of spirit.

'What we need is something red,' said Ian. 'That'll make him charge.'

That afternoon they met at the gate. Mark had his dad's waistcoat turned inside out so the red lining was showing. John had a red hanky and Ian had his mum's red underslip. But Morris wouldn't play. He flexed his muscles, lowered his head, stared at the underslip, lost interest and started to chew grass. Ian advanced with the slip held sideways in a bullfighting position.

'Come on, Morris, do a bit of a charge,' he said, dancing right up to him. Morris took a step forward; his huge bulk quivered at the slightest movement. Then the fat tongue came out, curled round a piece of the slip and the big yellow teeth started to chew.

'Give it back, Morris,' said Ian desperately.

They all had a tug. Ian even tried prising his jaws open, but slowly the underslip disappeared.

As Morris swallowed the last bit he turned and trudged back to the shade of his tree. Ian was so angry he followed him and clouted his huge behind. Morris's tail flicked round and caught Ian in the eye. He probably thought he'd just swatted a fly.

Morris was a very boring bull. He wouldn't charge, buck, bellow or even paw the ground with his hooves. So the boys went back to playing cricket, ignoring Morris, who stood under his tree being boring. Morris may not have been very bull-like, but he had the curiosity of a cat, so when the white Mini came through the gate and parked in his field he lumbered over to have a look. The man and woman who got out of the Mini noticed neither the sign warning them of Morris nor Morris himself. They'd spread their rug, brought out their picnic and were sipping a cup of coffee with their backs to their car when Morris arrived. Morris licked the Mini, but knew straight away he couldn't eat it. So he squeezed his huge head through the window to see if there was anything juicy inside. There was — a baby in a carrycot on the back seat. Fortunately Morris didn't notice the baby; but the baby noticed the big black horned head, the probing rough tongue and the yellow teeth. It started to cry.

'Now what's the matter?' said its mother, getting up from the rug. 'I'm sure I don't get a minute's peace with . . .' Then she broke off and began to scream — long, loud and hard. Morris panicked, tried to withdraw his head, got his horns stuck against the roof and did a real bull-like bellow. Then he lifted his head, and the Mini with it. The car was a metre off the ground when the boys arrived. The baby was yowling, Morris bellowing, the woman screaming and the man dancing around looking for a stick to clobber Morris.

'Put it down, Morris,' said Ian, poking his head through the other window. Morris's pink eyes saw Ian. He relaxed a little and stopped bucking. Ian put a carrot on the front seat. Morris lowered his head to sniff at it. The wheels of the Mini returned to earth. Ian climbed into the front seat, stroked Morris's head, and pushed the carrot between his teeth. Then Mark joined Ian and they began to twist Morris's head until eventually his horns came out of the car followed by his nose.

'Go back to your tree, Morris,' ordered Ian. And Morris did. He trotted away, as near to being in a rage as he'd ever been in his whole unbull-like life.

'Oh, you wonderful boy,' said the woman; she kissed Ian and wet him with some tears.

'It was nothing,' said Ian. 'It's not very fierce.'

'Not fierce. It looked nasty enough to me,' said the man who was white-faced and still shaking. 'You three deserve a medal.'

When the 'Courier' reporter asked for Ian, his dad looked alarmed.

'What do you want him for?' he asked.

'He's done something very unusual,' said the reporter.

Ian went off to be photographed with Morris. They tried for half an hour to get Morris to look fierce but with no luck. The reporter even suggested sticking a needle in him, but Ian wouldn't let him.

But when the story appeared in the 'Courier' — 'Brave Boy Beats Bellowing Black Baby-eating Bull' — Morris looked quite fierce in his picture. His mouth was open in a snarl. Only Ian and the reporter knew he was about to snap up a carrot.

'We are very proud of you,' said Ian's dad. 'I want to buy you a present. Anything you want?'

'I wouldn't mind a new cricket ball,' said Ian.

'Good lad,' said his dad. 'I'll get you one from town.'

'Where are you taking him?' Ian asked the girl.

They watched in disapproval as the lorry backed into

27

the field, the tail-board lowered and Morris fetched from his place under the tree.

'To stud in Devon,' said the girl.

'Will he be coming back?'

'Maybe — after he's killed a few more bullfighters.'

'He couldn't kill a baby rabbit,' said Mark.

'You've never seen him in a frenzy,' said the girl.

But Morris didn't look as if he could ever get in a paddy, let alone a frenzy, as he lumbered up the tail-board, making it bend with his great weight. His huge be-hind disappeared, then his swishing tail. He made a low mooing sound as the lorry started up. The three boys watched it disappear, hoping vainly that Morris would hoof the side out, and charge back to the field.

'He was more of a pet than a bull,' said John sadly.

'Let's get on with the game,' said Mark.

But they didn't play with any vigour, and after half an hour they trudged sadly home.

That night Ian looked up *stud* in Devon in his dad's AA book of maps, wondering if he could visit Morris in his holidays. It wasn't there.

'That girl's nothing but a liar,' thought Ian sadly.

Think It Over

1 How would the boys get first innings?
2 What was the message?
3 What does the bull do instead of charging?
4 What does the girl tell them about the bull?
5 How do the boys try to fool Morris?
6 How do the boys discover that Morris is tame?
7 What strange object does Morris eat?
8 How do the boys get Morris out of the Mini?
9 Why does the Courier reporter want Ian?
10 Where does Morris go?

Do You Know?

1 Does red attract bulls?
2 What silly thing do the boys do?
3 Can a farmer put a bull in a field with a public footpath?
4 What happens in a bullfight?
5 Do you approve of bullfights? Why?
6 Who might be the bravest of the boys?
7 What are cattle fed on in the winter?
8 Name three other small cars.

Using Words

1 'enormous' What other words do you know meaning very big? Make a list.
2 What single words would you use for: eat hurriedly g. . .; eat carefully and thoroughly ch. . .; eat daintily n. . .; eat enjoyably m. . .?
3 'spin like a catherine wheel' What else spins?
4 Adverbs telling you how something is done end in 'ly' quite often. Pick out six from this story and use each one in a sentence of your own.
5 Write these plurals: hoof h. . .; roof r. . .; proof pr. . .; loaf l. . . .
6 'underslip' What words do you know beginning with 'under'? Make a list.

Write Now

1 Write as a play what Ian's dad says to him when he learns he has been playing with a bull.
2 Write down in a short list the things you might do if you worked on a dairy farm.
3 Describe the most stupid thing you have ever done.
4 Write your own story called 'Chased by a Bull'.
5 Write a different headline for the 'Courier'.
6 Write two other 'Beware' notices.

The Hill

Sometimes, as Brock the badger plodded through his tunnels under the Hill, he felt the presence of the ghosts of animals and of men dead long ago. These were not frightening things. They protected him.

He did not know why. Neither he nor any living man could have turned back time four thousand years or more and seen the Hill as it was — a sacred place. Then, on one night of the year when the moon was full, long lines of men, women and children, dressed in skins and carrying torches would gather on the Hill. Each line would be led by its tribal priest, wearing the animal mask which was the totem of the tribe. That was the Night of the Beast-Gods. On that night, the tribes would worship the spirits of animals and pay their debts.

To us today the ceremony would be horrifying. To those skin-clad people it was just and right. They had killed animals for their food and for their clothing. Now they paid for the lives they had taken with a human life. One person from each tribe, drugged and unresisting, would be placed on the altar stone on the Hill and sacrificed to the Beast-Gods. That way man and animal kept a pact. No animal was ever killed on the Hill. No one in any of the tribes would have dared to do such a thing. The spirits on the Hill would have taken instant revenge.

Those tribes and their savage customs had long since passed from human memory. And yet, in all the centuries since, no road had been driven over the Hill; no house had ever been built there. Even today you didn't, if you were wise, go after the rabbits and the pheasants up there with a trap or a gun. People in the nearby village of Fulton said that that sort of thing 'didn't do you any good' and they had eerie tales to prove it.

The altar stone had sunk partly into the earth but the top of it, pitted by weather and mossed over, could still be seen. Brock had often scampered and scuffled around it in play with his fellow cubs on the summer nights of his youth.

Joe Rawlings seldom went to Fulton. He might have heard some of the tales about the Hill but he would not have believed any of them. None of them would have been in his mind that night. He had much more important matters in hand.

'All set?' he asked his brother, Marty, as he came back through the darkness.

'All ready,' Marty told him. The two men crouched at the entrance to the badger's sett. Joe sent one of the terriers in. They waited, clutching their spades.

Brock had had a good night's hunting before the prowling men had disturbed him. He had not seen them but there had been their scent in the air which had made him hurry back for cover. He had reached his tunnels on the Hill safely but there had been a strange feeling about them which made him feel uneasy.

He had not gone far before he stopped and snarled. Something was following him along the tunnel. The passage was too narrow to turn in so he scrabbled his way along to where it broadened out. There he swung round on the invader. The pitch darkness hid it but the smell of dog was unmistakable. It backed away rapidly. Brock snarled at it again. It kept its distance. Brock backed away satisfied to have scared it off. Badgers, though brave, do not attack without a good reason and only fight if they have to.

Then the dog started to creep towards him again and

he made a rush at it. The dog scuttled back and Brock continued his retreat. The dog advanced. Brock growled and went for it. Once more the dog drew back.

Brock grew angry. The dog wanted to keep him there. He could have driven it right out of the tunnel. But he could smell the harsh, frightening reek of the men outside and he did not want to go near them. He sensed that they were somewhere overhead. There was a scraping and a thudding in the earth above him. He could not work out what it was. His mind was taken up by the snarling threat of the dog.

He crouched, preparing to spring and waiting in silence for the dog to draw nearer once more. He knew he would have to move fast to grab it. Then the roof over his head fell in. The harsh scent of man filled the tunnel. Brock tried to scuttle backwards but the dog was on him, snapping and dodging the killing clamp of Brock's huge jaws, making the badger stand its ground.

Brock saw the real danger too late. Iron pincers reached for him and held him. He was pulled up into the air. A blow crashed on his head and a blaze of light flashed through his skull. Dazedly he felt himself lifted out of the sett. His jaws and legs were bound. He was lifted again. Rough, stifling material enmeshed him. His limbs thrashed desperately against it but he knew he could not escape.

The two men looked at the twitching sack in the moonlight.

'A good big 'un,' Marty judged.

'Aye,' Joe agreed. 'A boar. Wi' plenty of fight.'

The terrier had struggled out of the hole and now stood sniffing the sack cautiously.

'Let's get him in the van,' Joe ordered. The two carried the sack up the Hill, down the other side and across the wide scrubland to the Medford-Fulton road. Marty helped his brother to load the imprisoned badger into the back of the van.

'Eight o'clock tomorrow, then?' he asked.

'That's right.' Joe nodded. 'Yatt's barn.'

'Right.' Marty walked over to his motor cycle, started it and with a wave rode off towards Medford. Joe drove home in the van to the neighbouring town of Chadstowe.

Brock had been in the stifling sack for fifteen hours. Some of the time he had struggled and some of the time he had slept. He began to struggle again as rough hands dragged him from the van and carried him.

Light dazzled him as the sack was opened. His paws and his muzzle were cut free but before he could take advantage of that freedom he found himself falling and landed on his back. He was in a pit. The place reeked of men and dogs. A ring of men's faces, staring excitedly down at him, edged the pit. Then the dogs were released and came in, snarling and yelping, to the attack.

It was no easy victory. Brock was strong and courageous. His claws and jaws were deadly weapons. His thick coat armoured him. Twice the dogs backed off in a ring, showing their fangs in rage. But their blood-lust overpowered their fear each time. Brock, still clawing and biting ferociously, began to move more slowly. He was wounded in many places and most of the dogs would need stitching, too.

At last, his breath coming in thick, dragging gusts, he stood at bay. The dogs swarmed over him. There was a hectic din of growling and worrying. The heap of bodies heaved and writhed; Brock's head broke through, a dog's fangs fastened in his wet, red throat. Then the dogs covered him again. The heap heaved for the last time.

Rage and breath ebbed away from Brock; his agony lessened. His soul gave one last soundless cry to the spirits on the Hill. Then he felt nothing at all. The dogs were hauled off as he twitched and lay still.

All the dogs were bleeding; one was dead, another dying. But the men were talking excitedly to each other, praising their dogs and the dead badger.

Joe was grinning. He stuffed a wad of notes into his back pocket as he dropped into the pit with the sack. He held it open for Marty to lift up the corpse of the badger and drop it in.

'A grand bit of baiting!' one of the men called.

'It was that!' agreed another. 'When's next time, Joe?'

'Soon enough,' Joe told him. 'I'll have to find another brock first.' He pulled out the bundle of notes and began to count Marty's share into his outstretched hand.

Two nights later, Mary Rawlings awoke with a start. In the moonlight she could see her husband sitting up on the edge of the bed.

'What's up, Joe?' she asked sleepily. 'Worrying about Marty?'

Travelling home on the night of the badger-baiting, Marty had had a serious accident on his motor cycle. The news had been a shock to them both. Marty was still in a critical condition in hospital.

'No, not Marty,' Joe said thickly. 'I was dreaming. I was out in the open,' he whispered. He still seemed half asleep. 'There was a man among the trees. No — not a man. It had a man's body. But it had an animal's head.'

'Go back to sleep,' she told him. She wondered what had got into him. He had never been a man to be troubled by dreams.

'He stood there.' Joe made a reaching movement with his right arm. 'He waved to me. He was — beckoning.'

'Just a dream,' she yawned. The bed jerked and she sat up slightly. 'Where are you going?'

'Out. A walk,' he muttered in a dazed way.

'This time of night?' But she didn't argue. It was better not to with Joe. Her head sank back on the pillow. Drowsily she heard him go downstairs and out of the front door. Then the sound of his van starting dragged her awake again. She almost got up to call to him and ask him where he was going. But she thought better of it and slipped back into sleep. She regretted that afterwards.

'When I saw the van still parked there on the Medford road on the third day as I went to work, I began to think it might have been stolen. So I phoned the police.' Billy Dent who worked for a Fulton farmer was telling the tale in the Fulton Arms after the inquest. 'They told me that a Mrs Rawlings had reported her husband missing'.

'I went up the Hill to take a look. I found him easily. I thought he was asleep at first. He was laid out on his back on that big slab of stone up there.'

'And I'd noticed another funny thing before I got to him. The place was alive with animals. The trees seemed full of pheasants. They went up, flapping and squawking, as I disturbed them. There were a lot of rabbits about, too. And a fox. And a badger. I just caught a squint at him out of the corner of my eye before he disappeared. I always thought badgers only came out at night.'

'Anyway — he wasn't asleep. He was dead. They decided at the inquest that it had been a heart attack. There wasn't a mark on his body. The jury ruled out suicide or murder. I knew he was dead from the look on his face. His eyes were wide open and staring and his lips drawn back.' He paused and took another drink of beer.

'I've thought a lot about that since. There's nothing up there on the Hill to scare a man like that. He must have imagined he saw something as the heart attack took him. Maybe it was something he'd done that he suddenly remembered — something bad. I've never seen pure terror like that on anyone's face before. I stood there horrified.' He paused again.

'I'll say this,' he went on, 'from that look I'd judge that

whatever he'd done — whatever he had on his conscience — he'd certainly paid his debts.'

Think It Over

1 What did Brock feel protected him on the Hill?
2 What sort of place had it been four thousand years ago?
3 What did the tribesmen at that time think would happen to anyone who killed an animal on the Hill?
4 What stone still stood on the Hill?
5 How did Joe and Marty make sure that Brock would not go deep into his tunnels that night?
6 How did they pull Brock out of his tunnel?
7 In what place was the badger-baiting held?
8 How was Brock killed?
9 What happened to Marty Rawlings?
10 Who did Joe dream about?
11 On what stone did Billy Dent find Joe Rawlings' body?
12 What peculiar thing did Billy Dent notice then about the Hill?
13 What had been the cause of Joe Rawlings' death?
14 To whom, do you think, had Joe 'paid his debts'?

Do You Know?

1 Was Joe Rawlings a superstitious man or not? Give some evidence from the story for your answer.
2 What was the 'scraping and the thudding in the earth above him' that Brock heard in his tunnel?
3 Why did the two men tie up Brock's jaws and legs before they put him in the sack?
4 What sex is a 'sow' badger?
5 Why would some of the fighting dogs in the pit have needed stitching?
6 'His soul gave one last soundless cry to the spirits on the Hill.' What would Brock's last cry have been if it could have been put into words?
7 What might Joe have seen that frightened him to death?

Using Words

1 What is a 'totem'?
2 You will find these words in the story: presence; protected; unresisting; revenge; savage. Think of one word *opposite* in meaning to each of them and use each of your new words in a sentence of your own.
3 Write out the following, punctuating it correctly as speech:
   a grand bit of baiting one of the men called it was that shouted another when's the next time, Joe soon enough Joe told him I'll have to find another badger first
   Now compare your version with the slightly different one in the story.
4 'plodded' 'scampered' Find four other verbs in the story which describe how animals move, and use each one in a new sentence of your own.

Write Now

1 People in Fulton told 'eerie tales' about the Hill. Had a poacher or another kind of hunter had a strange experience there? Write your own 'eerie tale' about the Hill.
2 Write your own story about a ghostly animal.
3 Have you ever been alone in some place in a town or in the country that you felt was weird or frightening? Write about what happened there and how you felt.
4 Did Marty Rawlings see something that made him have his motor cycle crash? Or was there some other strange cause for his accident? Either in the form of a play or as speech, write out the conversation he has with a friend as he describes what happened.
5 Write a short account of your view of cruelty to animals giving some examples to show why you feel as you do.

Roovenge

The two men climbed out of the car and stretched their legs. They were obviously not agreed about the right dress for a long weekend safari into the Australian outback. The shorter, younger one wore long khaki shorts that clung to his podgy white thighs and were tied loosely round his slightly protruding middle. His companion, tall, thin and dignified, wore the same dark grey suit in which he had yesterday completed a deal with a Darwin firm. The deal would bring him and his colleague enough commission for fifty expeditions into the outback. Not that they were likely to want more than the present one, because even after only three hours' journey through the flat lifeless country they were both beginning to look hot and sticky and sound ill-tempered.

'What does it say, Jerry?'

The shorter man, Jerry Marston, had returned from reading a large roadside notice.

'Nothing.'

'You were a long time reading nothing,' said Alex Glew, wiping his sweaty forehead with a large white handkerchief. Alex was growing more unsure about the expedition every moment. Jerry was a good salesman, lively and knowledgeable, but socially he was liable to outbreaks of high-spirited stupidity.

'Untwist those long white knickers and relax, Alex. I meant it doesn't tell us anything we don't know.' Alex went to read the notice himself.

'Extreme heat, sand drift and other hazards beyond this point require special precautions,' Alex read out.

'So we made special precautions. We've enough water for three elephants and rations for a whole tribe of aborigines,' said Jerry.

'It says we mustn't leave the vehicle if we have a mishap.'

'Oh, get in the car or we'll never be back in time to catch the plane,' said Jerry.

They drove another hundred kilometres before hauling their hired camping gear out of the boot and dropping it on the carpet of needle leaves that had fallen from a stunted tree.

'This is a *Mulga* tree,' said Alex, referring to a guidebook he had bought in Darwin.

'Very interesting,' said Jerry, sarcastically. 'Get the primus going.'

Darkness came quickly. They suddenly felt quite cold. Alex put on a new pair of blue-striped pyjamas. Jerry sniggered and climbed into his sleeping bag without changing.

'I don't believe there are any damn kangaroos,' he said. 'Could they live in this God-forsaken place?'

'The whole point of them is that they can survive with little water,' said Alex, brushing his teeth with the little water he'd poured into his tin mug, and spitting it out under the Mulga tree.

'Anyway, we saw a lizard — not bad for a two-hundred-mile drive,' said Jerry.

'A *goanna*, it was called,' said Alex. 'I've just looked it up. In any case we've not just come to see the kangaroos. The whole landscape is remarkable.'

'It's that all right,' said Jerry. 'It's a remarkable lot of nothing. I wish I was in the hotel bar.'

But they slept well, and were in quite good humour when they set out in the morning through the barren lifeless landscape broken only by a few shrubs, the occasional tree and some unfriendly red sandhills.

Their eyes smarted from sweat and were so dazzled by
the shimmering heat that when Alex eventually spotted
the two kangaroos he at first thought it was a mirage.
'Look out,' he shouted.
'What's up, sport?' said Jerry, and stopped singing
'There was a wild colonial boy'.
'Kangaroos to starboard,' said Alex, now certain. The
kangaroos were obviously going to cut across the road,
at least a quarter of a mile in front of them.
'Step on it. I'll get the camera,' said Alex and turned
round to fumble in his rucksack on the back seat.
So Jerry stepped on it and the car shot forward over
the rutted track, emptying Alex into the back seat.
'They're going like trains,' said Jerry.
The kangaroos had seen them, but instead of turning
back, they increased their hopping speed and veered
right slightly to race across the road.
'Quick, get the camera out,' yelled Jerry.
'I'm trying to, you damned fool,' said Alex, scrabbling
about in the back seat.
'Hang on,' Jerry suddenly shouted and braked. The
car slid and skidded along the sandy track. Most of Alex
was spilled back into the front seat. When he had re-
gained his seat and his dignity, he saw only one kangaroo
hopping madly away to his left.
'Where's the other one?'
'I've run over it,' said Jerry sadly.
The kangaroo lay on its side. Its eyes were still open,
but glazed and unseeing.
The two men gazed sadly at its thin, furry body. It was
difficult to connect it with the frenzied hopping creature
that had tried to escape the car a few moments ago.
'Looks weird, somehow,' said Jerry. 'It's all tail, ears
and legs.'

40

'It's a terrestrial herbivore,' said Alex, who had his book open.

'Well, we bagged one,' said Jerry, suddenly recovering his spirits. 'Let's take a photo of one catch.'

Alex took two from different angles. Then Jerry started to be silly. He propped up the kangaroo, balancing on its tail and hind legs. Then he stood with his arm on its shoulder in the manner of a big-game hunter and invited Alex to take a picture.

Then it was Alex's turn. He was doubtful at first but then he thought a photo of himself as a kangaroo-hunter might impress his young son, Damian.

The sad-looking kangaroo head flopped on Alex's shoulder as he and Jerry swapped places.

'Looks like he fancies you,' said Jerry and giggled.

'Get on with it,' snapped Alex.

'Hang on a moment. I've got an idea,' said Jerry.

It took a few minutes to persuade Alex, but eventually he took off his jacket and the new floppy white hat that he had bought specially in Darwin for the safari.

'Hold him still,' said Jerry, 'while I dress him.'

So Alex stood behind the kangaroo, his feet astride its tail and held it upright while Jerry threaded its floppy arms through the sleeves of Alex's jacket. It was rather long so Jerry tucked the cuffs under until its forefeet showed through. Alex joined in the spirit of the joke and smoothed the jacket down its back. It nearly reached its tail. Then Jerry jammed the sunhat over its ears and stepped back to admire his handiwork.

'Just the job,' he laughed.

'Shall I hold it while you take the picture?' said Alex.

'No, let's prop it up so that it looks alive. That'll make a much better picture. We'll call it: "What the well-dressed kangaroo is wearing".'

So they experimented with the position of the kangaroo's feet and tail until it stood upright without support. Jerry carefully did up the two buttons on the jacket and adjusted the hat. Then Alex adjusted the camera to get the kangaroo into sharp focus.

'He looks great,' laughed Alex.

And then Jerry took a picture from a different angle. Just as he did so he thought he saw the kangaroo's head move but he decided he must be imagining it — perhaps the heat was affecting his eyes. But when, its slack body straightening, its tail moved and it did a short, experimental hop, he dropped the camera.

'Catch it; it's off,' he shouted.

But far too late. The men made a dive towards the kangaroo but it was twenty metres away before they could move. As it picked up speed the white hat fell off, but the grey jacket stayed firmly on, buttoned carefully by Jerry a few moments ago.

'Stop! Stop!' screamed Alex, waving his arms in a most undignified way and stumbling over the sand in desperate pursuit of the disappearing kangaroo.

Trying to outrun a kangaroo in its natural habitat, even one wearing a jacket, is like trying to outrun a greyhound round a dog track. The fat small man and the thin tall one returned hot and angry to the car.

'Should we try and drive after it?' said Alex.

'We'd get about twenty metres and then be stuck.'

'It wasn't dead,' said Alex.

'Now, that's very observant of you, old boy,' said Jerry. 'Ten out of ten for observation.'

'No need to be sarcastic. I meant it must have only been stunned. Now it's got my jacket.'

'What was in it?'

'Oh, Lord!' said Alex, feeling suddenly cold, despite the heat. 'There's my wallet with my money, travellers' cheques and . . . my passport.'

'Looks like you'll be taking out Australian citizenship, old boy,' said Jerry. 'I told you you should have dressed

42

more sensibly.'

'It's all your fault, you little fat fool,' said Alex, sitting sadly on the front bumper of the car. He was almost crying, his dignity totally gone.

'If it comes to insults, you look like a beanpole in red braces,' said Jerry. 'Why can't you wear a belt, like a normal person?'

Alex didn't reply. He put his boiled face in his long, thin hands and moaned. Jerry felt suddenly guilty.

'Cheer up, old boy. I've enough money to see us back.'

'You haven't,' said Alex.

'Sure I have. I've three hundred dollars at least.'

'The kangaroo's got it. He's also got your passport. When you gave me your stuff to lock away in the hotel I decided it would be safer in my wallet.'

Now it was Jerry's turn to despair. It was half an hour before either of them spoke.

'Maybe it'll come back this way,' muttered Alex eventually. My book says they use the same tracks to waterholes.'

'To hell with your book,' said Jerry. 'Let's get started back before we fry.'

Two days later the Darwin police were visited by two pink-faced unshaven English businessmen. One was wearing grey trousers and a blue-striped pyjama top.

'We're in trouble,' he told the desk-sergeant.

'You look it,' said the sergeant unsympathetically.

'We've lost our money and passports,' said the thin man sadly.

'Stolen?'

'In a way.'

'Where?'

'In the outback.'

'In the outback?'

'Yes, by a kangaroo.'

At first the sergeant thought they were drunk. A little later he decided they were mad. Two hours later when he'd taken them to have the film developed, he'd decided they were the best joke he'd heard in Darwin for the twenty years he'd been in the force.

'Can I borrow this?' he asked when he'd eventually finished staring and giggling at the jacketed kangaroo.

'What about our passports?' said Alex.

'Yes, well, we'll have to see what we can do. I'm just going to nip this round to a chap I know. I've got an arrangement with him. He's a reporter on the Darwin Gazette. I'll be back in . . .'

They didn't catch the last words. The policeman was in such a hurry to spread the good news.

'We'll be a laughing stock. "Poms grant kangaroo British citizenship" will be the headline,' said Jerry.

'We'll probably get the sack. It's all your idiot fault,' said Alex.

'At least if we do I won't have to work with a miserable streak like you again.'

Think It Over

1 How were the two men differently dressed?
2 Why were they hot and sticky?
3 What did the notice say?
4 Where were they going to sleep?
5 What have they mainly come to see?
6 What did Alex first think the kangaroos were?
7 How does Jerry start to be silly?
8 What do they dress the kangaroo in?
9 Why don't they drive after the kangaroo?
10 What was in the jacket pocket?
11 What does the policeman want the photo for?

Do You Know?

1 What is the Australian outback?
2 In what way don't these two men get on?
3 What is an aborigine?
4 How many miles is one hundred kilometres?
5 How does a kangaroo travel?
6 Which way is starboard? What is the opposite?
7 What is a big-game hunter? What do you take with you if you hunt big-game now in a safari park?
8 What other animal is Australia famous for?
9 What is the famous Australian song?

Using Words

1 Explain the title of this story.
2 What does 'herbivore' mean? What does 'carnivorous' mean?
3 What is a 'pom'?
4 Use each of these difficult spellings in a sentence of your own: disappearing; colleague; handkerchief; occasional.
5 A kangaroo can be called a 'roo'. Give a slang name for: a horse; a cat.
6 'ill-tempered' Find the other hyphenated words in this story. Use three in sentences of your own.

Write Now

1 Write the headline that appeared in the 'Darwin Gazette'.
2 What is the most embarrassing thing that has happened to you? Write a few sentences about it.
3 Write a story called 'Lost in the Desert'.
4 Make a list of equipment you would need for a three-day camping expedition.

Catching an Alligator

As usual he didn't tell us what it was for until it was finished.

'Now,' he said, looking with satisfaction at the muddy pool and grassy bank we'd spent almost a week enclosing with a primitive fence, 'that should keep him in.'

'Keep what in, Mr Waterton?' I asked.

'The alligator, of course. Didn't I tell you we were going to catch an alligator?'

'A live one, sir?'

I know it was a silly question, but the idea of the two of us fishing an alligator out of the river and inviting him back to spend a few days in our pen while we studied him shocked me into asking it.

'Of course a live one, boy. Is the heat getting to your brain?'

If the Brazilian heat was getting to my brain, it must have long ago penetrated his. Hadn't I seen him, a few days ago with my own eyes, calmly moving leaves and twigs following the fat body of a fourteen-foot coulacanara snake, looking for its head? And then when the huge head was revealed didn't I see him calmly undo his trouser braces, lie flat along the body and tie up the hissing jaws with them? It had taken me and three Indians he had hired to carry the huge snake back to our hut coiled round a long pole, while he marched behind, singing 'A hunting we will go' and holding up his trousers with his large hairy hands. If anyone was mad, it was *him*.

Still, you couldn't help liking him. I'd always been a keen naturalist, and so when I had a chance to go on a

South American expedition with the famous Charles Waterton, I jumped at the chance. That was two years ago, 1871, and I suppose I'd do it again — with him. With anyone else I'd never have survived the Brazilian swamps, jungle, diseases and, most of all, the animals. We'd now recorded at least twenty specimens previously unknown, and gathered more data on the well-known ones. I trusted him, although I knew he was slightly mad and would risk anything in his passionate desire to record every form of animal life in the continent.

'How are we going to catch an alligator, Mr Waterton?'

'With great difficulty, boy. But we'll do it, won't we?'

'If you say so, I suppose.'

'Nil desperandum,' he said and showed his large white teeth in a grin. He was always quoting Latin at me; I didn't understand a word of it.

For two days we fished for an alligator with a lassoo, a thirty-feet length of strong rope, dark as the river so that the alligator couldn't see it. I began to lose my faith in him. How could he expect to lassoo an alligator standing on the muddy bank of the river? But he had hawk eyes as well as a hawk beak of a nose and could spot the huge dark backs of the toothy creatures when they cruised near the surface.

It was mid-afternoon on the third day of our hunt when he suddenly yelled 'Got him', and ran a few yards up the bank unwinding the rope.

'Hold this, boy,' he commanded, 'and I'll go and fetch some pullers.'

'But what if . . .'

'Don't argue; just hold on. If he pulls just let the slack go and follow him upstream. It's only like playing a fish.'

'Except that . . .'

I was about to say that there weren't many fishes as big as alligators but he'd disappeared already, running excitedly in his big black boots as if he were a boy who'd caught a tadpole. There was no movement on the rope; I held it slack, but my hands were sweaty with tension.

Ten minutes later he appeared with three Indians from the creek and the chap they called Daddy Quashi, the negro from Mrs Peterson's. Of course he hadn't told them what he'd caught; otherwise they wouldn't have come. Then he explained that he'd got an alligator on the end of the rope and he wanted them to pull him out of the water. They stared at each other, then at him. He could see they were about to bolt, so he promised each of them five dollars.

'I'll get a gun. We'll shoot him, sir,' said Quashi.

Of course that set him off shouting and threatening to throw poor old Quashi to the alligator. I explained to Quashi that he needed the alligator alive.

The three Indians walked away a little and held a whispered meeting. Then they came back and said they'd do it if he'd allow them to shoot a dozen arrows into the alligator, to disable him.

'Do you think I've come three hundred miles to get an alligator specimen for you to spoil!' shouted Mr Waterton, and the Indians were silent.

Then Daddy Quashi made a run for it. Waterton chased him, rugby tackled him about a quarter of a mile into the scrub and hauled him back.

'Best do it,' I whispered. 'I think he's more dangerous than the alligator.'

Waterton distributed five dollars to each of the Indians and Daddy Quashi. Then he showed them the long Spanish knife that he kept hidden in his tunic. I don't know whether they thought it was for them or the alligator, but it calmed them all a little and they agreed to pull the rope.

'Fetch the mast from the canoe,' Mr Waterton ordered me. It took me some time to remove it. As I carried it back along the muddy bank I wondered what he was going to do with it. It was about eight feet long and the thickness of my wrist. When I handed it to him he crouched by the water's edge, the mast held in the same position as a soldier holds his bayonet.

'Now lads,' he began, like a general addressing his troops, 'we're going to catch an alligator. I'm between you and him. If he tries to snap me up, I'll give him this mast to chew on. One, two, three pull,' he yelled and we did.

It was only when I saw the threshing water that I knew for sure he'd really lassooed the alligator. His scaly back appeared on the surface; then he thrashed and plunged and dragged all four of us towards the water.

'Pull for your lives,' shouted Waterton, still crouching with his mast, ready to feed the alligator.

It would have made more sense to shout 'Run for your lives', but we were still as afraid of him as of the alligator, and none of us dared to be the first to drop the rope. After a minute's straining we got him to the surface again; then his head appeared on the bank, two yards from the crouching Waterton. The alligator was angry and afraid. His body and tail were threshing and plunging; I could even see his mean little threatening eyes. Then he opened his jaws to snap up Waterton. I'd never seen an alligator that close before. His jaws were enormous. His long rows of sharp teeth looked sharp enough to chew up the canoe mast as if it were a matchstick.

'Do something, you madman,' I thought to myself, as the enraged alligator was pulled to within two feet of Waterton's head. If it plunged forwards instead of pulling back, Waterton was doomed. Suddenly Waterton leapt to his feet and threw the mast aside. He never intended using it; it had only been a device to comfort us. We were so amazed at what he did that we almost dropped the rope. He vaulted onto the alligator's back as if it was a horse, turning half round as he jumped, so that he was facing the right way.

'Tallyho,' he yelled and seized the alligator's forelegs, twisted them up his back and hung on to them as a bridle. The alligator plunged, furiously lashing the sandy part of the bank with his large, powerful tail. But Waterton, sitting near his head, was out of reach of both tail and jaws. As the alligator was pulled completely out of the water he started to buck as well as twist and slash, but Waterton held onto him like a broncho rider.

The Indians and Daddy Quashi cheered excitedly. I joined in. My confidence in Mr Waterton was restored. We made so much noise that we didn't hear him shouting his instructions.

'Whoa there,' he yelled, waving his arms. This released the alligator's front legs and it started to make some progress towards us, even with its ten stone rider.

'Another rope,' yelled Waterton.

This time I heard him, and ran for the spare rope in the canoe.

Fifteen minutes later the alligator was making slow but steady progress towards his temporary home. Daddy Quashi and two Indians were leading him by the rope fastened to his head while the other Indian and I held onto a rope round his tail. If he speeded up towards Quashi and the Indians we had to brake him by pulling on his tail. Actually he didn't cause too much trouble. He was puzzled and defeated; he still didn't understand how he'd been outsmarted and was probably wondering when the weight from the sky would fall on his neck again.

Waterton was already making notes as he walked beside his captive. If Daddy and the Indians pulled too hard Waterton would yell, 'Carefull of his scales; damage him and you'll be his tea.' We were all very careful – you could never be sure that Waterton was joking – so the alligator reached his stockade undamaged.

Before we let him loose Waterton measured him from nose to tail as calmly as if he was measuring a wall.

'Thirteen feet, five inches,' he announced and recorded it in his book.

Later in the day I would have to record the details more neatly while he wrote another chapter of his book *Wanderings in South America*. But that wouldn't be until it was dark. Waterton never wasted a moment of daylight. Once released the alligator disappeared into his pond.

'Let's leave him for now,' said Waterton. 'I want to catch a spider monkey before dark.'

I followed him reluctantly. Perhaps he would ask me to swing through the trees making noises to attract a spider monkey for him to dive on. If so, I'd have to do my best. Whether or not he was mad, he was certainly interesting and somehow I felt safe with him.

'Did you know I rode three years with Lord Darlington's foxhounds, boy?' he asked suddenly.

'No, sir,' I muttered.

'I used to think it was a waste of time. You never can tell. It was good practice for riding the alligator.'

Think It Over

1 What was the fence for?
2 How was the snake caught?
3 Why did Mr Waterton seem mad to the boy?
4 How are they going to catch the alligator?
5 How does Mr Waterton persuade the Indians to stay?
6 What is the mast for?
7 What surprising thing does Mr Waterton do?
8 How many ropes are there attached to the alligator?
9 How are the ropes used?
10 How does the boy think he might have to catch the spider monkey?
11 Where has Mr Waterton learned to ride?

Do You Know?

1   What century does this story take place in?
2   When did zoos start?
3   What does a naturalist do?
4   Name a famous one from television.
5   What is the difference between an alligator and a crocodile?
6   Name one disease you might get in a jungle swamp. It begins m . . .
7   Who normally uses a lassoo?
8   What is a creek?
9   Name three countries that still have jungles.
10 Who would normally shout: 'Tallyho!'?

Using Words

1   What words would you use to describe a swamp? Make a list.
2   'Brazilian' What would you call an inhabitant of: Australia; Mexico; Kenya; Norway; India; Sweden? Which is the odd one out?
3   What other occupations end in 'ist'? Make a list.
4   'Nil desperandum' What does this mean? Where can you find out if you don't know?
5   Use 'bolt' in two different ways in sentences of your own.
6   Use 'scales' in three different ways in sentences of your own.

Write Now

1   Describe what it feels like to pull on a tug-o-war rope.
2   Using your swamp words write a piece called 'Jungle Swamp'.
3   Write a poem called: 'Alligator' or 'Snake' or 'Monkey' or 'Night in the Jungle'.
4   In a few sentences describe the most awkward thing you ever moved.

Gelert

Legend tells of a man once great in Wales. His name was Llewellyn. He was chief in the land and he ruled his people well. Though he was just and kind, he had a quick temper and tried to keep it in check.

The dearest thing Llewellyn owned was his dog. Gelert was a wolfhound and worthy to belong to a great chieftain. He had a wise look on his face and his tail was like a knight's plume. He was a strong and handsome dog who could run all day when he was hunting and bring down a stag or a wolf at the end of it. No thief or enemy would ever have dared to creep up on Llewellyn while he lay sleeping if Gelert slept by his side. Yet, though Gelert was as brave as a lion and as deadly as a dagger-thrust, he was great-hearted enough to be gentle with creatures who were weak or young. Children might scramble on Gelert's back or pull his ears or his tail. He would stand blinking mildly or twitching his hide at too sharp a pull. But he would never snarl or snap.

Fate was both kind and cruel to Llewellyn. For many years he had been childless and he and his wife had longed for a son or daughter. Then, at last, the gods granted them a son. Llewellyn rejoiced in the small boy and seemed to live for nothing else.

One of the wise men at Llewellyn's court warned him against Gelert. Dogs, the wise man said, were jealous animals. Every day Gelert could see the love his master gave to his new son. Gelert would feel himself forgotten and he could be dangerous. He could harm the little boy. It would be better if the hound was put away.

Llewellyn rejected this angrily. He said that he would stake his life on Gelert's loyalty. The wise man went away, aware once again of how quickly Llewellyn could be made angry.

Then dark days came and such things passed from people's minds. Llewellyn's wife was very ill. After the birth of her son she had seemed to recover but then she caught a fever. She had never been strong and in spite of all the careful nursing she received she grew weaker day by day.

After her death, Llewellyn was a grim and silent man. He kept to himself, brooding on his loss and racked with grief. Gelert was his only companion, sharing his master's sorrow. Only when he saw his son did Llewellyn's sadness seem to grow less.

At last he could stand it no longer and called for his horse and weapons. He would escape from his memories by going hunting alone. His courtiers tried to reason with him. If he intended to hunt, he ought to hunt in company. It was wild weather and the wolf packs were prowling. He told them that he welcomed danger and rough weather in his present mood and he needed none of them. But he would take someone with him. It was the only company he could stand at that time – his little son. The courtiers were horrified but they were timid. None of them dared to argue with Llewellyn.

They watched him set off on that late autumn morning. His son, wrapped warmly, was safely clasped in Llewellyn's arm. Beside his master's horse trotted Gelert.

By midday Llewellyn had found what seemed like good hunting country and he made camp in a ruined hut. The wind blew through the doorway and the windows but Llewellyn's mind was too sunk in sadness to notice the cold.

He was not careless about his son, however. He had

brought a cradle for the child and clothes to cover him
warmly. When the boy was sleeping, Llewellyn told
Gelert that he would have to stay behind that day.
Gelert's ears drooped slightly but he made no attempt to
follow Llewellyn and lay down obediently on guard beside the cradle.

At dusk, Llewellyn came back. He had had no success
with his hunting and the howling of wolves made him
urge his horse along faster, though he thought his son
would be safe enough in Gelert's care.

He entered the hut and stood like a man turned to
stone. The words of the wise man thundered in his head.
The cradle was empty. The rags of the bedclothes,
covered in blood, lay scattered across the floor. In the
dim light, a great grey ghost, stood Gelert. Blood spat-
tered his coat and dripped from his jaws.

Llewellyn did not look for his son, sure that he would
find only a lifeless body, dead at the fangs of a jealous
and treacherous dog. Gelert had betrayed him and killed
the child.

Llewellyn's heart seemed to swell with grief and rage
until he choked. As Gelert stepped towards him, he drew
his sword and struck. Gelert died in silence.

Time, then, had no meaning for Llewellyn. It could
have been minutes or hours that he stood there. What
roused him was a faint, frail sound. The colour drained
from his face. It had been a baby's cry. Was his son still
alive?

The child was not only alive but quite unharmed and
in his search of the room Llewellyn found something
that made his heart stand still again with shock. It was the
corpse of the largest and most savage wolf Llewellyn had
ever seen in his life. Intending to attack Llewellyn's son,
it had met the brave and faithful Gelert and its own
death.

Sadly, Llewellyn comforted the child, wrapped him

warmly and carried him safely home. Then, as he rode, Llewellyn wept for his dead wife and the wickedness of his own untrusting and angry heart. But, most of all, his tears fell for Gelert who had been true-hearted and valiant to the end.

Some say that this is only a legend and that there was never such a dog as Gelert. But, if you travel from Caernarvon to the foot of Snowdon, you will come to a place where the dog and its name are remembered. The place is a village called Beddgelert which, in English, means the Grave of Gelert.

Think It Over

1 What bad fault of character did Llewellyn have?
2 In the beginning what was his dearest possession?
3 How did Gelert behave towards children?
4 After many years what stroke of good fortune did Llewellyn have?
5 What did one of his wise men say about Gelert then?
6 What ill-luck happened to Llewellyn after that?
7 How did Llewellyn hope to escape from his grief and his memories?
8 How many companions did he take with him and who were they?
9 Why did Gelert not go with Llewellyn when he went hunting?
10 What scene met Llewellyn's eyes when he returned to the hut?
11 How did he react?
12 What two things did he find after that to make him bitterly regret his action?

Do You Know?

1 What evidence in the story is there that it happened a long time ago?
2 Besides having a quick temper, in what other ways was

Llewellyn a man of strong feelings? Give some reasons from the story for your answer.

3 In the light of what happened later, what dangerous advice was Llewellyn given?

4 Can you name another town or place in Great Britain that has a story or legend attached to it?

Using Words

1 What is the difference between a chief and a king?

2 Where would a knight's 'plume' be worn?

3 What does 'as deadly as a dagger-thrust' tell you about Gelert?

4 'He said that he would stake his life on Gelert's loyalty.' Write out, punctuating the speech correctly, the exact words that Llewellyn said. Begin, 'Llewellyn said . . .'

5 'racked with grief' Give another word which means almost the same as 'racked'.

6 'a cradle' What are babies put to sleep in nowadays and how is that different from a cradle?

Write Now

1 Are you sorry for Llewellyn or do you think he brought his troubles on himself? Give your view of his character and give your reasons for your opinion of him.

2 Write your own story, which could be real or imaginary, about a dog.

3 Have you ever regretted being angry with someone? Write about what happened. *Or* write your own story about a person whose quick temper got him or her into trouble.

4 In play form or as speech write the kind of conversation that Llewellyn's courtiers might have had as they talked about the dying queen.

5 If there is some local legend or story in your area, write a short account of it.

Saved from the Circus

It was hotter than usual in a teak wood forest deep in Burma. Timba, the herd leader, was about to finish work; he was near the end of his five-hour stint. He dragged his last huge tree trunk to the river, twisted it round with great skill, gave it a push with his forefoot, and watched it tumble down into the river. His mahout patted him on the head. But Timba knew that his work was not finished. After twenty years in the forest he knew when logs were going to jam. He sensed it before his mahout. But he was not sorry. He would get into the cool river before his daily bathe. His skin itched with excitement.

He slid down the bank, careful not to tip his mahout in. Soon he was shoulder-deep in the water pushing with his forehead, using his immense strength to get one hundred logs on the move with the current again. He had no tusks to help him with his task for he was a hine. This was why he was leader of the herd. Tuskless elephants are stronger. They can pass their trunks under a foe's tusks and either throw it down or break off a tusk.

It took him a quarter of an hour. But now his day was over. His mahout rode him to a shallower part of the river and scrubbed him with rough bark and coconut husk which pleased him greatly.

The other elephants came to join him. Soon there were twenty of them. Manu, a great heavy female known as a 'koonkie' (an elephant that trained other elephants in the art of moving timber), came down with her baby, Simla. She had been on light work since giving birth.

Simla had already learned how to roll and get her whole body wet in the water.

After half an hour the elephants left. Not unwillingly, for they were now moist and their skins had stopped itching and they knew rations of salt, the fruit of the tamarind tree and other nourishing foods awaited them.

After their meal they were set free till the next morning. They did not wander too far because they dragged after them a heavy chain which slowed them down and left a trail for their mahout to follow next day. But they trumpeted with the pleasure of their freedom.

Mr Rawlings, the head forester, was glad to see Manu wander off without her baby. Her mahout had been detailed to play with it and the ruse had worked. It would be easy now to lead Simla to the railway station. He did not want to sell her; he hated parting with elephants. But the owners of the forest had made him strike a deal with the owner of a German circus. They were looking for a baby elephant to train. They were also buying other animals in the area and had chartered a special train of caged trucks which was now standing in the station.

Manu was now well hidden in the trees and it was easy for the mahout, with a bagful of tamarind fruit, to coax Simla along to the station train. Soon, again bribed with fruit, she was in the caged truck and the circus owner stood prodding her. She would be a great attraction in the circus. Children loved baby elephants. Next morning they would be off to the circus five thousand miles away.

Manu was uneasy. She had not seen her baby for four hours. She had gone back to the feeding ground and to the river, but she could not find her. She trumpeted to Timba who could sense her distress but did not know the cause of it.

Darkness comes suddenly in Burma. The circus owner had left the station and gone back to his camp in the village. While the men had been with her Simla had been calm in the caged truck thinking it was some kind of game. Now they were gone she realised that she was trapped. She let out a great shrill trumpeting. To her surprise no man came to free her. She now began to panic and rock from side to side against the bars of the truck.

An elephant fears no one, and so his sight, sense of smell and hearing are not well-developed. But a mile away in the forest Manu picked up the vibrations of Simla's call. She lumbered over to Timba and nudged him. He could feel her distress and lifted his head. Now he too picked up the distress calls of Simla, his daughter.

The night was split with his huge bellow. Moving as fast as his chain would allow him he set off in the direction of the calls. Manu followed close behind and then came eighteen other elephants attracted by the bellow.

Mr Rawlings and his men were at a party in the village.

'The elephants are noisy tonight,' said a mahout. 'Should we go and look at them?'

'No,' said Rawlings, 'it's probably a fight. Better keep out of the way until it is over.'

Once free of the forest the elephants moved at great speed despite their chains. They were all in line behind Timba. Smelling her mother, Simla's cries became very loud so the elephants were guided easily to the caged truck. Timba seized an iron bar in his trunk on one side and Manu did the same on the other. They pulled and strained. At first the bars held but the elephants' training in the forests had given them great patience. The bars began to bend and finally to snap.

While Timba and Manu were trying to free Simla the other elephants went on the rampage through the station. It was built of wood and corrugated iron and offered little resistance to their heavy bodies and the dragging chains. The noise woke the circus owner in his camp. He rushed with his men to the station. 'My animals!' he screamed. 'These elephants must be shot.'

As his men raised their rifles Mr Rawlings dashed on the scene. 'Stop!' he yelled. 'Do not shoot!'

'But my circus train. There are thousands of pounds worth of animals in there.'

'My elephants are worth a great deal more.'

While they argued Timba had pulled harder than Manu and tipped the cage truck over. Now they were kicking with their great forelegs at the wooden roof. Soon it was smashed. Simla rolled out, unharmed. Timba gave a great trumpeting shriek. He turned back towards the forest. The others followed, Simla hanging onto Manu's tail with her trunk. Some chattering monkeys had also been released.

'My animals!' screamed the circus owner. 'I will report this to the Government.'

'Report it to who you like', shouted Mr Rawlings.

As dawn rose Simla was playing with her mother. Timba was by her side. Mr Rawlings gave them the day off to settle down. At sunset he washed Simla himself.

Think It Over

1   What kind of wood grows in the forest?
2   What does Timba spot before his mahout?
3   Why is the elephant keen to get into the river?
4   What kind of elephant is Timba?
5   How is an elephant washed?
6   Why do the elephants not go far when they are free?
7   Why was Simla separated from her mother?
8   How did the mahout get Simla to the station?
9   What does Manu do when she finds Simla gone?
10   How did Simla try to get out of the truck?
11   Why did Rawlings not go and see what was the matter with the elephants?
12   How did the elephants get Simla out of her caged truck?
13   Who stopped the circus owner from shooting the elephants?

Do You Know?

1 What are elephants' favourite foods?
2 What wood is teak? Hardwood or softwood?
3 Why were the logs in the river?
4 What is a koonkie?
5 Why must an elephant be washed frequently?
6 Where in the world are there still wild tigers?
7 What, in this story, shows that an elephant is intelligent?

Using Words

1 What do you call a group of elephants?
2 An elephant trumpets. What noise do these animals make: a lion; a dove; a wolf?
3 What different names are there for types of horses?
4 'tuskless' What does 'less' added at the end of a word do?
5 Give two other words meaning 'ruse'.
6 'forelegs' What other 'fore' words do you know where 'fore' has been put in front of an existing word?

Write Now

1 In a few sentences describe what it is like to walk through a wood or forest on a hot day.
2 Write sentences about these animals working hard: a cart-horse pulling a brewer's dray up a hill; a horse in the Grand National; an ox pulling a plough. Underline any words that show that the work is hard.
3 Suppose the circus owner began to shoot. Write as a short scene of a play what happened.
4 In a few sentences describe how you feel before and after you get into a swimming pool on a hot day.

62

The Winner

'And Bob will be back on Monday with your new friend,' said Malcolm's father. Malcolm was five. He hadn't liked Bob from the moment he first came bumping up the track to his house in a green truck. Malcolm's father had introduced him as Robert Turner. Malcolm had said 'Hello, Mr Turner,' and offered to shake hands, as he'd been taught. Bob had ruffled his hair instead, laughed in his high-pitched voice with his pin-head thrown back and said, 'Just call me Bob, boy.'

Malcolm had sat listening to his father and Bob. He hadn't understood all of their conversation, but had gathered that Bob was a member of a group of scientists at a university. He said 'primates' a lot and 'essential research'. It seemed Malcolm's house was the perfect 'environment' for carrying out this 'essential research' and that Malcolm was at the 'right stage of development'. Bob then measured Malcolm against the wall and said he was exactly the right height for the 'experiment'. Malcolm had a vague idea that 'experiment' meant cutting things up and had a bad dream about Bob cutting off his arms and legs, laughing and saying 'Just call me Bob.'

But when the green truck arrived the next Monday Bob climbed out, not with a set of saws and knives, but with a chimpanzee. He led it up the driveway and stopped in front of Malcolm and his father.

'This is Zimba,' said Bob. 'Say "hi" to Zimba, Malcolm.'

'Hello,' said Malcolm, staring at the hairy little creature. Malcolm had only seen pictures of chimpanzees. They looked different close up. 'What enormous ears he has,' thought Malcolm, 'and what a wide mouth, and what long arms.'

'Shake hands with Zimba,' said Bob.

Malcolm wondered whether to ruffle his hair and say 'Just call me Malc,' but decided it was safer to do as he was told. He took Zimba's hand and shook it slowly three times. The hand felt rough, but Malcolm noticed the hand had the same number of fingers as he, although the nails on the ends were much longer.

'Physical contact should be encouraged wherever possible,' said Bob, but Malcolm didn't hear him. He was already showing Zimba the kitchen. He liked him much better than he liked Bob.

Malcolm's family ate their evening meal on the verandah as usual. Malcolm's mother, as usual, complained about the heat. Malcolm never really understood the complaint; his family had left England before his first birthday so he had known nothing except the hot humid African climate all his life. His father sat at the head of the table and his mother and sister at the sides. Wedged together at the bottom end sat Malcolm and Zimba. Zimba didn't sit much. He kept climbing from his chair and hiding under the table. Malcolm's father kept fishing him from his hiding place and returning him to his chair. Malcolm didn't think his mother liked Zimba; his father kept saying they were making a 'significant contribution to research into primates', but his mother pulled faces at his sister and remained silent. Zimba pulled faces as well: Malcolm pulled faces back at him. Zimba was the first friend he'd had.

Zimba did many things Malcolm had been told not to do. For instance, he didn't use a knife and fork. He scooped up his food and made a mess on his face and the floor. Nobody told him off. In the end Malcolm started eating his potatoes with his fingers, as he'd always wanted to do.

'Use your knife and fork,' said his mother sharply, and she gave his father a nasty look.

Malcolm took up his knife and fork reluctantly. It wasn't fair. He looked jealously at Zimba. Zimba pulled a face that made Malcolm laugh. Malcolm did his best cross-eyed look and pulled his ears sideways, like Zimba's. Zimba made a hooting noise; Malcolm hooted back. His mother and sister left the table.

At nine o'clock it was bedtime. Malcolm had to wash and get into his pyjamas. Zimba didn't have to do either, and Malcolm felt another pang of jealousy. They sat side by side on Malcolm's bed while his father read them *Peter Rabbit*. Malcolm knew the story and kept joining in. Zimba listened for a few minutes and then grew restless. He wiped his face with Malcolm's bedsheet. Then he put his long hairy arm round Malcolm's shoulder and fell asleep just as Mr McGregor was chasing Peter Rabbit with a hoe. Malcolm wondered how Zimba could go to sleep in such a frightening part of the story. Malcolm's father tucked Zimba up in the bunk next to Malcolm. Malcolm could see his wide black face sticking out from under the sheet. He fell asleep trying to flare out his nostrils by screwing up his mouth and blowing short, sharp bursts of air down his nose. When he woke Zimba was still sleeping. Malcolm heard his father washing in the bathroom. He wondered what Zimba would look like if he soaped him all over and shaved him with his father's razor. Perhaps he'd try it when he knew Zimba better.

The good thing about Zimba was that he was useless. At ping-pong Malcolm beat him 21–0 in the first game and was leading 7–0 in the second when Zimba chewed the ball up. Then Malcolm challenged him to draughts. Zimba tried very hard but he was no match for Malcolm. His chief fault was that when Malcolm moved one of his draughts Zimba simply moved it back. Malcolm explained to him that he was only allowed to move the black ones, but he didn't seem to understand. In the end Malcolm made his moves for him, and beat him easily.

What annoyed Malcolm was that, although it was obvious he could beat Zimba at everything, people always took more notice of Zimba than they did of him – especially Bob. Take rolling cars along the lounge floor, for instance. Zimba wasn't too bad at this, but Malcolm knew he was better. They would face each other sitting crosslegged three metres apart. They each had three cars, and the game was to see if you could get all six at your opponent's end at the same time. When they had first played this game Zimba had cheated. He threw the cars rather than rolled them on their wheels. But in the end he decided to play fair, and could roll them back to Malcolm almost as quickly as Malcolm could roll them to him. But he was lazy. After a few rolls Zimba would pick up a car, stare at it and chew it. Then Malcolm would whizz all the cars down to Zimba's end and win. Bob watched them doing this for an hour, and wrote things in a notebook. But he always wrote about Zimba, never about him. One day Malcolm threw the cars at Zimba and Bob scowled at him.

But when no one was watching Malcolm enjoyed playing with Zimba. He never seemed to mind losing. He lost at football, cricket, rugby, ping-pong, cars, marbles, draughts and three-card brag. Malcolm's funny Uncle Sidney had taught him three-card brag and when he'd gone Malcolm's mother had tried to unteach him it. But he remembered the rules well enough to beat Zimba. The only game Zimba didn't lose was darts. Malcolm declared it a draw because Zimba wouldn't wait for Malcolm to pull his darts out of the board before he started pelting his. Also a dart had got stuck in the ceiling and Malcolm knew that *he* would be blamed.

Then one day a taxi arrived to take Malcolm and Zimba to school. Malcolm had been looking forward to going to school before Zimba arrived but now he wasn't so sure. The school was four miles away in the town and Malcolm had noticed on shopping expeditions with his mother that there were many big, dangerous-looking children milling about in the playground. Still, he thought, as he sat in the back of the taxi with Zimba, their arms round each other's shoulders, there would be at least one person in the school he could beat. When Malcolm's father took him out of the taxi and left Zimba in, Malcolm couldn't believe it.

'Why can't Zimba come?' he asked, beginning to cry.

'Because he's a chimpanzee,' said Malcolm's father.

'But he's my friend,' wailed Malcolm.

'At home he is; at school you'll have to be without him.'

And there was nothing Malcolm or Zimba could do. Zimba whimpered and pulled faces and struggled to follow Malcolm. Malcolm wailed and wriggled to try to get back into the taxi with Zimba. But Malcolm's father and the taxi-driver were too strong for them.

At home Malcolm told Zimba all about school. Zimba nodded and grimaced and seemed to understand, especially about the bigger boys who could read, write and play football even better than Malcolm. Then Malcolm would play football with Zimba and win easily and feel better. Malcolm wished the school was full of Zimbas.

One Sunday morning Malcolm and Zimba sneaked out of the house and went for a walk. Normally they were only allowed to play near the house, but Malcolm's mother and sister had gone to church and his father was having a boring conversation with Bob. Bob said the experiment was 'reaching a satisfactory conclusion' and Malcolm felt worried because he now knew that 'experiment' didn't always mean cutting up; sometimes it meant

Zimba. He also knew that 'conclusion' meant 'finish' so he had a vague fear that Bob might cut Zimba up. Malcolm was so worried he didn't notice how far they'd gone until they reached the clump of trees, half a mile from the house, and strictly out of bounds.

'We'd better turn back,' said Malcolm. But Zimba didn't want to. He let go of Malcolm's hand, leapt onto the lower branches of the largest tree, and sat there pulling faces and whooping at Malcolm. Malcolm decided to follow him. He leapt for the lowest branch – and missed. He got up and tried again – again he missed. He couldn't understand it. Zimba wasn't supposed to win at anything. Malcolm pushed a stone against the tree, stood on it and, after much struggling and damage to his knees, managed to haul himself onto the lowest branch. Then he clambered up to the branch where Zimba sat chattering happily. As soon as Malcolm reached Zimba, Zimba coolly and easily climbed another three metres. Malcolm began to be afraid. He wanted to go down. But how could he? If Zimba won Malcolm would be shamed for the rest of his life. He struggled bravely on. Zimba even pulled him from one fat branch to a much thinner one.

'I can manage,' said Malcolm, but he wished his legs would stop shaking. Stage by stage boy and chimp climbed the tree, the chimp always ahead, gibbering excitedly. Painfully, slowly, and fearfully, Malcolm followed. After thirty minutes, chimp and boy sat side by side on a branch six metres from the ground.

'A draw,' Malcolm explained to Zimba. But Zimba was going for his first win. He stood up on the branch, put his hand on a thinner one above, and swung to another two metres away. There he sat whooping and grimacing. Malcolm tried to stand but his legs wobbled. Then he managed to grasp the branch above. He bent his knees like Zimba had done, shut his eyes and leapt.

Zimba climbed down the tree slowly. He sat by Malcolm's body for a long time. He moved the stone that Malcolm was resting his head on. He tried to pull him up by the hand. It was all no use. Zimba sadly climbed back up the tree and hid until he heard the voices of Malcolm's father and Bob.

At the inquest the coroner said that, although he understood the necessity of research into primates, in this case far too much attention had been paid to the effects of the boy on the chimpanzee and far too little to the effects of the chimpanzee on the boy.

Bob said afterwards that the coroner was typical of the small-minded petty authority which wants to shackle those who seek to extend the frontiers of knowledge. Malcolm's father said nothing; nor did he speak when he reached home. There was no one to speak to. His wife and daughter had left him and gone back to England.

Think It Over

1 Why did Malcolm instantly dislike Mr Turner?
2 What was Malcolm's bad dream?
3 What first strikes Malcolm about the chimpanzee?
4 Why can Malcolm stand the African heat?
5 Does Malcolm envy the chimpanzee at the table?
6 What story does Malcolm's father read him? Does Zimba listen?
7 What is Zimba like at games?
8 Why is Malcolm afraid of going to school?
9 Why does Malcolm wish the school was full of Zimbas?
10 How does Zimba finally beat Malcolm at something?
11 How does the experiment finally go wrong?

Do You Know?

1 What kinds of animals are used for experiments?
2 What do you feel about some of the experiments done to animals?

3   What does 'environment' mean?
4   What does a coroner do?
5   In what ways are chimpanzees like humans? Can you list three ways?
6   In what ways are they different? Can you list two ways?
7   Where would you find a verandah on a house?
8   Should chimpanzees be allowed to advertise tea? Is it insulting to them?
9   How might the tea adverts be made?
10   Do you know any people who imagine intelligent things about their pets?

Using Words

1   What is Bob short for? What are these short for: Bill; Dick; Liz; Kate?
2   What are these other chimpanzee-like animals? Can you spell them correctly? g. . .; b. . .; m. . .; a. . . .
3   'a significant contribution to research into primates' With the help of your teacher put this into simple language. Is it always best to use big words?
4   Use 'draughts' in two different ways in sentences of your own.
5   What noises do young children make while playing with toy cars? How would you write them down?
6   What three noises does the chimpanzee make in this story? h. . .; g. . .; w. . . .

Write Now

1   Write a story in which an experiment on an animal or animals goes wrong. It could be: 'The Big Rats.'
2   If you filmed this story for TV, what shots would you want of the final scene in the tree? How would you show Malcolm's thoughts?
3   Write a letter to a newspaper complaining about the use of animals in experiments.
4   Describe what it is like to climb a tall tree.

70

Manhood

Greg had not done much work at school that day. Miss Dupré had told him off three times. But there was a restlessness in the village. The restlessness that came before the great seal hunt. He was thinking about the seal hunt. The weather was twenty below now; all fishing on which the community depended had stopped because it was too dangerous among the ice floes. Now they depended on the seal hunt to get them through the winter.

When he was a man he would go on the hunt. In the summer vacation his father had let him go on short fishing trips, not long ones. His mother would not let him be away long; she had lost his brother at sea. It was great to be out there with the men.

When the bell went he was surprised to see his father outside the schoolroom. 'Hello, fella,' he said. 'How's your right arm?'

'What do you mean, Pa?'

'It had better be strong because it's going to be awful sore by the end of the week.'

'You don't mean...?'

'Yes, we need an extra hand. Your Uncle Douglas has cut his arm real bad. I guess you're strong enough. You're thirteen and growing like a pine.'

He began to run. Then he stopped. Men don't run. He tried to stroll home casually with his father but it was all he could do to stop himself from leaping.

He slept very little that night. First there was his mother arguing with his father. He heard his name mentioned. Then he was shivering with excitement. At the bottom of his bed were the furs he was to wear next day getting warmed. He wiggled his toes into them. At four-thirty his father had said. But at four on his watch he heard his father stirring so he rushed to dress.

'I guess you look the part,' said his father. 'Coffee?'

'Sure.'

'Now you eat this, son,' said his mother bringing in a great plate of bacon and beans with thick crusts of fried bread.

'I ain't hungry, Ma.'

'Now you eat good,' scolded his father. 'Where we're going there ain't much time for fancy meals.'

But it was hard to get the food down, especially with his mother fussing round him. 'You will look after him, Reg.'

'Don't fret. Our Greg here's nearly six foot. He can take care of himself.'

Now he was in the back of the wagon. There was that special smell of men he had smelt on the fishing trips, partly of stale tobacco.

'Want a chew, kid,' said one, handing him a plug of tobacco.

'Now don't you get him no bad habits. And not so much of the kid.'

Greg was pleased that he said that, but he would have liked a chew of tobacco so he could spit like the men.

The journey was mainly through dark pine forests. Canada sure was a big country. It was dark again by the time they reached the shack on the edge of the ice floes.

He did not sleep at all that night. He was lying on hard boards and the temperature was down to thirty below. Even though the men had let him sleep by the stove he was freezing down one side.

At four they all got up. His father made a breakfast of beans and coffee. Then they were in a boat nudging their way in the dark among the ice floes.

Soon he could hear a mewing sound. The men's faces came alive. It was the harp seals. During the breeding season they came in from the big ocean onto the ice floes of the Canadian and Newfoundland coastlines to have their pups. It was the pups that must be killed within ten days of birth. Then their pelts were soft and white and could be sold. The fresh meat was also saleable back in the villages when there was only frozen food to eat.

'When I say jump,' said his father, 'jump'. The boat was crunching up against a floe of ice. This was the dangerous part. If you fell in you would have to be taken back to dry out and the men would curse you; or worse you could get trapped under a floe and drown.

But he made it. His father patted him on the back and handed him his hakapik. This was a gaff to club the seals with. He swung it; it was quite heavy.

Around him he could see the white baby seals in the semi-dark light. He could not see the mother seals at first because their coats were darker. The pups looked cuddly and sweet like white teddy bears, but he knew they must be killed. The mewing sound echoed across the floes.

His father took him up to a baby seal. 'Right,' he said, 'you hit it three times on the skull. This puts it deeply unconscious. They tuck their heads in but you hit it right on the button.'

There was a thud and a slight crack as his father swung the club down onto the brittle skull. 'Ain't moving,' he said. 'I'll skin it.' He took his knife and ripped it up the underbelly and began to peel it off like skinning a rabbit. 'Now' he said, as he flung down the bleeding carcass, 'you kill 'em and drag them over there, and I'll do your skinning for a bit. You can practise that later.'

So this was it. His manhood had begun. He swung the hakapik; it hit the seal on the side of the face. It mewed loudly. He tried again and knocked out an eye. The mother seal came for him but his father kicked it aside and gave the baby seal its death blow. 'Try again,' he said. Greg's stomach was churning, partly from his failure and partly from the sight of the seal's hanging eye.

Soon he became more successful. It took him six blows. But by ten o'clock he had got it down to five and after the break at lunch time he got it down to four. His dad made him take rests. None of the men took rests apart from the lunch break. They slaughtered through the day until ten o'clock at night. By then Greg was asleep almost on his feet. His father took him to the boat.

The next thing he knew it was four-thirty and the men were getting ready. His right arm was as stiff as the hakapik. It ached from shoulder to finger tips. But this was being a man; he must get used to it.

Before they left, his father made him skin a seal. He was not good at it. He got blood everywhere. He felt like a kid again from the glances of the other men.

The same routine followed that day. The men were working silently. As soon as the sun came up you could see trails of blood across the ice. The wind moaned about them all the time, the seals mewed, and the clubs and hakapiks thwacked down.

He clubbed and dragged the corpses across the ice to where his father was skinning. Sometimes a seal would come round after being dragged and he had to club it again. Sometimes his father would skin a wriggling body.

His arm was too painful and swollen for him to sleep well that night despite his utter tiredness. As he lay he saw the faces of the baby seals and a mewing rang in his ears. If this was being a man he did not like it.

The next day his father tried to teach him to skin again but his right arm was too swollen and sore to do it properly. It was like a nightmare. He felt that he was a murderer or executioner each time he swung the hakapik.

The hunt lasted five days. Then they drove back to the village. He said nothing about his feelings.

'Cat got your tongue?' his father said kindly.

'No, Dad.' He just could not tell his father how he felt. The men would laugh at him as a baby. But the faces of the seals would not go away from his mind. He felt he would be haunted by them for ever.

'Cheer up. Have a plug of tobacco. You've earned it.'

He fell into a fever when he got back. As he lay sweating it out he could hear his mother and his father arguing. 'I told you he was too young.'

'He's got to learn to survive here. He did real good. He's a man now.'

The faces of the baby seals spun before him. '*Was* he a man?'

Think It Over

1 Why was Greg excited?
2 Why had the fishing stopped?
3 Why cannot Uncle Douglas go on the seal hunt?
4 What does his mother feel about Greg going on the hunt?
5 Why does Greg not want to eat his breakfast?
6 What is the first sound of the seals?
7 Why do the seals go on to the ice floes?
8 Why are the pups killed?
9 What was the danger in jumping out of the boat?
10 How do we know that Greg is unskilled at seal killing?

Do You Know?

1 Do you know another reason why seals are killed?
2 When would you say that you reached manhood or womanhood in this country?
3 What does twenty and thirty below mean?
4 Why might Greg have fallen ill?

5   What dilemma does Greg face at the end of the story? Was he too young to go on the hunt?
6   Should *any* animal be killed?
7   Have you ever thought of being a vegetarian? What common foods could you not eat?
8   What are the people who try to stop whaling called?
9   What is your opinion about sealskin products? Do you know any?

Using Words

1   'Cat got your tongue?' What does this mean? Complete these other animal expressions: as blind as a . . .; as sick as a . . .; to be . . .-headed; an . . . never forgets; as crafty as a barrow load of . . .
2   'schoolroom' What other words have 'room' attached without a space between? Check your answers.
3   What evidence in the speech is there that this story is not taking place in the British Isles?
4   'hakapik' What other names do you know for wooden clubs including sporting ones?
5   Write a list of words meaning 'to kill'.
6   What is a carcass? Does it sound nice to eat?

Write Now

1   Write a few sentences to describe what it feels like when you have a fever or a high temperature.
2   Using the facts from the story, plan a TV advert against seal hunting.
3   Write a poem called 'Seal Cull'.
4   Write a story called: 'The Animals Take Revenge.'
5   Write the argument between Greg's father and mother as a play.
6   Describe what it feels like to work physically hard.

The Hunters

Effortlessly, Kree soared on the invisible waves of the air. He was about a mile inland from the cliffs and the nest, where his mate, Irka, waited.

At that height, he could see the roof of a lonely cottage about another mile further inland. For a moment he felt the old familiar fear of man. But nothing moved outside the building and his hunting instinct was stronger than his fear.

Just below him was a small wood, a dark green patch against the moorland. Kree circled, watching. A pigeon flapped out from one of the trees and began to make its way across the shallow valley. Kree's wing-beats quickened; when the pigeon was out in the open, he swooped.

The pigeon sensed the attack and tried to change course. But it was too late to avoid that slate-grey lightning. Kree, travelling at over a hundred miles an hour, struck the pigeon as it swerved. Under the shock of the impact, it died instantly. Kree, with his killing talons fixed in its limp body, flew home.

Irka greeted him impatiently, taking the pigeon from him to tear at it. He perched on the narrow ledge, ignoring her and staring out across the sea. A long way off, a boat rocked gently on the silky, unruffled water. Kree gazed at it with fierce, yellow eyes.

He was not the only one watching the boat. To the north, where grass sloped down to a rocky beach, Donald Mackay was sitting. He was a large man in his sixties, grey-haired, with a craggy, lined, brown face. Two trout, wrapped in leaves, lay beside him. He was studying the boat through a pair of battered, old field-glasses.

'Yon's the man, Jock,' he said quietly. 'I reckon he's after them.' His dog, a mixture of breeds, cocked its ears and looked at him as if it understood.

The man in the boat, Harry Fenton, was also using binoculars. They were trained on the peregrine falcons in their nest on the cliff. Harry Fenton was about thirty, dark-haired and thin-faced. He smiled as he put the glasses back in their case. He was whistling as he started the outboard motor and began to take the boat back to the little fishing village of Ancaig lower down the coast.

At the noise Kree fluttered his feathers and stalked up and down the ledge. He was ready to take his turn at sitting on the nest and to let Irka go and do her own hunting. But she did not move, perhaps because the eggs were almost ready for hatching. He took the remains of the pigeon to the end of the ledge and began to eat.

In Ancaig, Harry Fenton returned his hired boat, went into a phone box and dialled a London number.

'Mr Perroni? It's me – Harry. I know where to get the birds you want.'

'How many?'

'Two – I should say,' judged Harry.

'Good, when?'

'I could get eggs now.'

'No,' said Mr Perroni. 'Get me the chicks. Deliver them safe and sound and there'll be a bonus.'

'How old?'

'Give them a month,' Mr Perroni told him. 'Take care.' He rang off.

As Fenton drove away along the only road into Ancaig that evening, Donald Mackay watched him go.

In the next few days the peregrine chicks hatched out into balls of fluffy down with ever-open, greedy beaks. Kree and Irka, untiring grey-blue wings against the sky, ranged the area for food. There was no satisfying the chicks but for Irka and Kree there was an animal pride in rearing them, something like love.

Donald Mackay watched them with pleasure. He felt that he and the peregrines had much in common. Like him, they took what they wanted from nature freely and confidently. Unlike him, though, they had never been in trouble for poaching.

You would not have got many good reports about Donald Mackay, if you had asked about him in the village. He had been a drinker and a fighter in his youth. Landowners did not like him at all. He would take trout or grouse or other game as if they freely belonged to him. Valuable salmon disappeared from streams visited by Donald. These he either ate himself or sold to hotels who didn't ask where the salmon came from. The money helped out with his pension. He was a tough old man who always went his own lonely way. He knew as much about the country around and its animals as any man could. If the rest of civilisation had suddenly disappeared, Donald would have survived.

Just over four weeks later, Harry Fenton came back to the district. From his pinnacle of air, Kree watched him set up his green tent. It vaguely disturbed him, as the things of man usually did, but he had the chicks to feed and ranged on with his hunting.

Harry had been careful to keep his arrival secret. He had come as darkness was falling and parked his car in a spot hidden from the road. He pitched his tent, too, in a hollow where it would not be easily seen. He had plenty of provisions and no need to go anywhere near Ancaig. It would be easy money, he told himself. He would get the peregrine chicks and then, with all the loot Mr Perroni would give him, he could have a month's holiday somewhere in a plush hotel.

That night Donald Mackay watched until he saw the light go out inside Harry's tent. Then he went home to his cottage.

He was up before dawn. He had to wait some time before Fenton stirred. He watched the man have his breakfast and then set off for the cliff top carrying an iron stake, a coil of rope, a hammer and a small canvas sack. Out of sight, Donald followed and, still out of sight, he watched Fenton hammer the stake deep into the ground at the top of the cliff. Fenton secured the rope, flung the loose end over the edge and then, with the sack on a string round his neck, he went to the brink.

Kree and Irka from the air could see both men. They forgot their hunting. A sick sadness and fear of what was to come filled them both. For Kree it was as if darkness had suddenly covered the sun. The long, exhausting hours of hunting, the weeks of care, had gone for nothing. He sensed it. They were going to lose the chicks.

As one of the men started to climb down the cliff, Kree and Irka began to fly round, crying out in agony.

That did not worry Fenton. Age-old terror of man and perhaps their knowledge that it would be hopeless to attack would keep them away. Peregrines would never attack man. He could see the chicks on the ledge below him. It was going to be an easy climb down.

Then he looked up and his bones turned to water. A face, grim as death, was staring down at him. Poised over the rope at the cliff, a knife glinted.

'You'll find a quick way down, if I cut this,' Donald said.

'What do you think you're doing?' Harry yelped. Was the man mad? His hands were suddenly wet and slippy.

'Come on up or you'll find out,' Donald ordered.

Harry looked down. 'You could kill me!' he gasped.

'Aye,' said Donald. 'Very likely. Come on up.'

Harry scrambled up the rope and stood trembling on

80

the cliff top, speechless at first with rage and fear. He watched Donald untie the rope and fling it over the cliff. Just for a moment, seeing his hammer on the ground, Harry wondered if he could grab it and knock the old man cold. Then, seeing the power in Donald's wide shoulders as he heaved and tugged at the deep-driven stake, pulled it free and flung it after the rope, Harry discarded the idea.

'You...! You...!' he spluttered.

'Now – get away out of it,' Donald commanded, pitching the hammer, too, into space. 'Don't come back. I'll be watching.'

Jock, sensing his master's mood, snarled at Fenton.

'I'll have the police on you!' Harry stammered.

'Do that,' said Donald. 'They'll be interested to hear you were stealing peregrines. It's against the law, laddie.'

'You old . . .!' Rage choked Fenton. Jock took a prowling step towards him. He turned on his heel and stamped off, the empty canvas sack flapping foolishly against his chest.

At a distance, Donald followed and watched as Fenton furiously packed up his tent and other belongings, loaded the car and drove off with a squeal of tyres.

When the noise of the racing engine had died, Donald gazed out across the moorland towards the sea. The falcons were still there. He nodded, pleased.

He knew that the fate of the chicks might still hang in the balance. In their confusion of terror and grief, the parent birds might fly off and leave them.

But Kree and Irka were staying. The horrible moment when they might have lost their young was fading from their short memories. Instinct was again responding to the chicks' hungry call. Irka and Kree were about to return to their hunting. The chicks would grow and fly without further threat.

Donald watched the peregrines circling against the

blue sky and murmured, 'Grand birds, Jock, they're grand birds.'

Jock wagged his tail in reply and followed his master as Donald began to make his way back to the cottage where the body of an illegal pheasant hung in the pantry, waiting to be plucked and cooked.

Think It Over

1   What was Kree hunting at the start of the story?
2   Was it a windy day or not? How can you tell?
3   Who else, besides Kree, was watching the boat?
4   Who was in the boat?
5   What message did Harry Fenton give Mr Perroni?
6   When did Mr Perroni want the chicks delivered?
7   How did Donald Mackay add money to his pension?
8   Why did Harry Fenton try to keep his return to the district a secret?
9   Why did he have the small canvas sack round his neck as he climbed down the cliff?
10   What threat stopped him from taking the chicks?
11   What happened to all his equipment?
12   Why didn't he attack Donald Mackay when he got back to the top of the cliff?
13   Why was Donald Mackay anxious when Fenton left?
14   What would Donald Mackay have for his meal that night?

Do You Know?

1   Who do you think lived in the lonely cottage mentioned at the beginning of the story?
2   Why would a trip in a boat be more helpful for Fenton's purposes than a walk along the top of the cliffs?
3   What does a peregrine falcon look like? (There are some clues in the story. If, however, you want to go into detail, you could look at a book of British birds.)
4   Why do you think Mr Perroni wanted the peregrines?
5   Another falcon in this country is much more common than the peregrine. Name it, if you can.

6   Name three kinds of bird that are shot for eating in this country.

7   What other eggs and nesting places of British birds are protected by law?

Using Words

1   Think of one word which means *the same as* each of the following: familiar; swooped; talons; fierce. Use each of these new words in a sentence of your own.

2   The meanings and the first few letters of the following words from the story are given. Write the words out in full, checking your spelling by finding the words in the story.

a) field-glasses   bin...

b) walked in a stiff or menacing or stealthy way   st...

c) an extra payment, more than expected   bon...

d) the highest point or peak   pin...

3   'Under the shock of the impact, it died *instantly*.' Use each of the following adverbs in a sentence of your own: impatiently; freely; confidently; vaguely.

Write Now

1   When Harry Fenton tells Mr Perroni he cannot get the peregrines, how would Mr Perroni react? In play form or as speech write their conversation.

2   Write your own story about the trapping of some animal. It could be set in this country or abroad. It could be from the viewpoint of the human trappers or from the animal's viewpoint.

3   A gamekeeper sees Donald Mackay going into a wood with his dog and follows. Does he catch Donald poaching or does Donald outwit him? Write the story.

4   You may have flown in an aeroplane or imagined yourself flying like a bird. Write a poem called 'Flying'.

The Great Dog Race

Scowler Morton had a black collie dog called Basil. It was big, fat and bad-tempered, just like Scowler. It chased cats, bit visitors and one afternoon scratched Alan Postgate's leg when he, Scowler and Steve Earl were collecting wood for their bonfire.

'That dog's dangerous. It ought to be put down,' said Alan, rolling up his trouser leg to inspect the damage.

'Serves you right. You should have given him some more,' said Scowler.

'He's had nearly half of it already,' said Alan, angrily. 'I didn't buy a bar of chocolate to feed Basil. Besides, he's fat enough already.'

'Fat! You calling my dog fat!' said Scowler.

'Well, you couldn't call him slim,' said Steve.

If there was going to be an argument, he was on Alan's side. Basil was a nuisance wherever they went. Last week he'd killed one of Mr Gibson's chickens and they'd all had to run and hide in the barn for two hours.

'He's one of the fastest dogs in the district,' said Scowler, his moon face beginning to light up with rage.

The other boys sniggered but pretended that they were coughing when Scowler turned on them with the only piece of wood he'd collected so far.

'Basil would beat your Flossie any day,' said Scowler, waving his piece of wood dangerously near Steve's head.

'Only at eating chocolate,' laughed Steve.

'Do you want to bet?'

'Bet what?'

'That Basil can't beat your loopy dog Flossie in a race,'

said Scowler.

Steve hesitated. Flossie was the most mongrel of mongrel dogs. Perhaps it was because she was made of so many sorts that she seemed confused. She tried to go through shut doors, down small rabbit-holes and up tall trees. She had a high-pitched bark that made the milkman suggest that there was a bit of cat in her as well as half a dozen different types of dog. Steve had never tried her at running, but she was so useless at everything else that he suspected the worst.

'You're scared,' sneered Scowler, as Steve hesitated.

'Course I'm not. It's just that I haven't any money to bet with at the minute,' said Steve.

'Don't you worry your little head about that,' said Scowler. 'Your fishing-rod against my new cricket bat. Are you on or are you too scared?'

There wasn't much option for Steve. He knew Scowler had wanted his fishing-rod for a long time. Now it looked as if Basil was going to win it for him.

'What about me?' said Alan. He'd bandaged his leg with his dirty handkerchief and was studying it to see if any blood was seeping through.

'I don't think you'd be much good against two dogs,' sneered Scowler, 'especially with a bad leg.'

'I'll bring my dog,' said Alan, trying to sound casual.

'You haven't got one, you liar,' said Scowler.

'That's what you think.'

'It's what I think as well, Alan,' said Steve. 'You've never said anything about having a dog.'

'That's because I only got it last week,' said Alan, studying his bandage to avoid looking at the other two.

'What sort is it?' said Scowler, suspiciously.

'A little Labrador,' lied Alan.

'O.K. Bring it along, if you've really got one. Don't worry, Labradors can't run,' Scowler said to Steve. 'It probably won't even beat your daft Flossie.'

'I'll bet my football,' said Alan rashly.

'Looks like I'm going to have a sporty year,' laughed Scowler.

The race was fixed for the next Saturday morning. Scowler said this was to allow time for training. In Alan's case it would also allow time for finding a dog. The one he had in mind was a big Labrador called Rufus who lived two houses away. He knew Rufus's owner slightly. He'd seen Rufus running after sticks and rubber balls, at least as fast as Basil and certainly faster than Flossie, who in Alan's opinion was a no-hoper.

'I wonder if Rufus would like to come for a walk . . . I've nothing to do and my mum suggested . . . Does Rufus want some exercise . . .?'

Alan rehearsed what he'd say to Mrs Thornton all the way home.

The next day Scowler and Steve were out in the park training their dogs. Alan watched them gloomily from a bench. He'd been to see Mrs Thornton but she'd not been very encouraging. Rufus had spiked his front paw in the rosebushes and was sitting by the fire feeling sorry for himself. However, Mrs Thornton said he could be taken for a walk when he was better. Alan just hoped he would be better for Saturday.

Scowler had a bag full of meat, scraps stolen from his dad's butcher's shop. He put a piece under the big chestnut tree and showed it to Basil. Then he dragged him back on his lead about fifty metres, got out a big stop-watch and let him go. Alan had to admit that for something so big, fat and hairy Basil could lollop along at a good pace. After three races for meat, Scowler looked at his stop-watch and shouted triumphantly, 'He's getting faster!'

'You mean fatter,' said Alan, but he suspected it might be true.

The next practice run cheered Alan up, though. When Basil was about ten metres from the meat an Alsation nipped round the tree and gobbled it up. Basil put on his brakes like a dog in a strip cartoon, but slid along the wet grass and stunned himself on the base of the tree.

'Get out, you ugly great brute,' shouted Scowler, puffing up towards the Alsation and brandishing his stick.

'He's nowhere near as ugly as you,' piped a little lady in a pink hat as she appeared from the other side of the tree dragged by the Alsation's lead.

'He stole my dog's meat,' shouted Scowler.

'He shouldn't have left it lying about,' said the lady. She dragged the Alsation back towards the path, muttering, 'Call my lovely doggie ugly, did he! And him with a face like an undercooked pudding.'

Basil recovered in time to see the Alsation turning back his head to make a sneering sort of bark. Basil gave a half-hearted bark back, and hid behind the tree. He had enough sense not to tangle with an Alsation.

'I'm taking him home to rest,' said Scowler as he passed Alan. 'There's no need for him to train really. You haven't got a dog whatever you say and a clockwork mouse could beat that thing.'

'That thing' was Flossie. Steve had been trying to run her alongside him on a lead, but she was like Goofy, rubbery-legged and flopping all over the place. In the end she did run a few paces – round Steve's legs. He fell in a heap and as he lay cursing, Flossie licked his face with her big tongue.

'Might as well give me your fishing-rod now,' called Scowler. Steve didn't answer. He picked up Flossie as if she was a rag doll and stalked off with her.

At nine o'clock on Saturday morning Alan approached Mrs Thornton's house, knocked nervously, shut his eyes and said a little prayer for the recovery of

Rufus's spiked foot.

'Is . . . is your Rufus in?' he asked, and went red because it sounded so silly.

'Yes, but I'm afraid he's not better. He's still feeling sorry for himself. But don't worry . . .' she went on quickly, seeing Alan's disappointed face, 'Uncle Harold's come for the weekend and he's brought Ingrid so you can take her for a while.'

When Alan saw Ingrid he felt quite dizzy and had to steady himself against the sideboard. Ingrid was a miniature poodle with a silly blue coat round her body.

'Woof,' squeaked Ingrid somewhere underneath her hairy white head.

'I've just remembered I've got to go on an errand,' said Alan.

'Just the thing,' said Mrs Thornton. 'Make sure she keeps on the path.'

Before Alan had recovered his wits he found himself in the road leading a midget dog in a blue coat on a silver lead. His first thought was to drop the lead and run. His next, more sensible thought, was to hide with Ingrid in the garden shed for half an hour and then take her back home. Before he could have any more thoughts there was a loud wheezing, choking noise behind him. He turned to see Scowler and Basil. Basil was staring at Ingrid. Scowler was leaning against the signpost doubled with laughter. Scowler got his name because he'd never been seen to laugh. Now he couldn't stop and it was not a pretty sight.

'Where do you put the batteries?' gasped Scowler when he had recovered enough to speak.

'These dogs are faster than they look,' said Alan bravely.

They set off for the park, a little white dog, a big black one, a small boy with an embarrassed red face and a fat boy who had to stop every ten metres to let out a series

88

of sniggers. Alan ignored the sniggers and the comments.

'Hope they've cut the grass short or you'll never find that thing once its lead's off.'

'If it were a dog-throwing contest you'd win easily.'

Of course there was quite a long pause while Steve finished laughing. Flossie licked Ingrid and then flopped on her as if she was an egg that needed hatching. Ingrid woofed once or twice in a friendly sort of way but didn't seem insulted, even when Steve asked if she was going to race on legs or wheels.

Then Scowler explained the rules. It seemed that in a proper dog race there was a hare and a starting gate. Scowler had tried in vain to borrow Mr Harby's white rabbit, so he had decided to be the hare himself. He'd tied a long piece of string to his trouser belt. On the end of the string was a big meaty bone, specially stolen from his dad that morning. When the starting gate went up, Scowler would run by it trailing the bone. The first dog to catch the bone was the winner. Alan and Steve had to admit that Scowler's starting gate was good. It was three enormous cardboard boxes he'd got from a shop. He'd stored them in the lower branches of the chestnut tree overnight and luckily no one had stolen them.

'The dogs are not supposed to see the hare – or bone – till the gate goes up. Then they suddenly see it running – or moving away. That shows how quick their reactions are, you see. So we put each dog under a box and you two pull the boxes up when I run past. At the same time – make sure of that. That's why there's a string handle on each box. So one of you can lift two boxes. Got it?'

'You seem to have worked it all out,' said Steve sulkily; he was now sure he could say goodbye to his fishing-rod.

'I don't want you two yelling that it isn't fair when you've lost,' shouted Scowler. 'Still I did make one mistake.'

'What?' asked Steve.

'I should have brought a shoe-box for Alan's dog.'

'Just get on with it,' said Alan angrily.

Basil went under his box so easily that Alan and Steve suspected he'd even been trained at that. Ingrid could go for quite a long walk under hers so she wasn't too unhappy. But Flossie was in trouble. Once you'd got one bit pushed under another bit stuck out, first a leg, then a tail and finally an ear. She was also making whining noises, not liking what she thought was a new game.

'If she comes out before I whizz past, she's disqualified,' said Scowler, and lumbered to his starting position.

You could hardly say Scowler whizzed along but he was going a fair pace for a fat boy when he passed the boxes.

'Now,' said Steve and released Basil and Flossie.

Basil was off after the trailing bone with surprising speed. Flossie was as angry as she'd ever been and lolloped after him, probably thinking he had put her under the box. When Alan lifted up his box he found Ingrid pretending to be asleep, as she had to every night when the light was put out.

'Come on, you stupid animal; you're an embarrassment,' said Alan giving her a push.

Scowler ran his fastest, head back like he'd seen proper runners on the telly. In fact he was outdistancing Basil. Then Basil caught up suddenly. Runners with their heads back should stay on running tracks, not run in parks where there are bits of wood and stones and low-hanging lime tree branches. As Scowler's head caught the branch it stopped; but his legs kept going. He looked as if he was taking off, but then the whole fat lot of him flopped to the ground. Basil sniffed him to see if he was dead. Flossie, still very cross, caught up with Basil and bit him. Basil yelped and, by now very confused, bit

Scowler's leg. Everybody knew then Scowler wasn't dead because he swore loudly. Then he remembered what should have happened.

'The bone; get the bone, Basil,' he yelled. 'It's at the end of the string.'

But it wasn't. The string dangled boneless and frayed from his trouser belt. Fifty metres further back a little white dog in a blue coat stumbled over a lump that smelt good. Ingrid stretched her jaws as wide as if she was in a dentist's chair and picked it up.

Alan laughed, Scowler swore, and Steve wondered if he could swap Flossie for a new fishing-rod.

Half an hour later there was a knock at Mrs Thornton's door.

'Had a good walk?' she smiled.

'Yes thanks, very good,' said Alan.

'She's a grand little dog, isn't she?'

'Oh yes, she is that,' said Alan.

'I see the errand was to buy a cricket bat,' said Mrs Thornton. 'Funny time to buy a cricket bat in October.'

'They don't cost so much out of season,' said Alan.

Think It Over

1   What kind of dog was Basil?
2   What did it do to Alan?
3   What is Steve's dog called?
4   What items were bet?
5   Who owned Rufus?
6   How does Scowler train his dog?
7   How does the little lady describe Scowler's face?
8   What does Alan feel about taking Ingrid for a walk?
9   Why does Scowler say 'I hope they cut the grass short'?
10   Who is going to act as a hare? How?
11   What are the boxes for?
12   What happens to Scowler?
13   Who won the race?

Do You Know?

1 What kinds of dogs race?
2 What do they race after?
3 How does Scowler's nickname suit him?
4 How much food should you give an average-sized dog?
5 What is the silliest bet you have made? Did you lose?
6 What do adults bet on mostly?
7 How would you train a dog to run fast?
8 Which dog name in this story seems the most stupid? Do you know any stupid dog names?

Using Words

1 Make a list of nicknames in your class. Are any insulting? Is it fair to give somebody an insulting nickname?
2 'sniggered' What other words are there for 'laugh'?
3 'loopy' What other words are there for mad? How many are slang words?
4 Use 'seeping' in a sentence of your own.
5 Which type of dogs begin with capitals in this story and which with small letters? Can you see any reason for this?
6 'dad's butcher's shop' Why are there two apostrophes?
7 Use 'train' in three different ways in sentences of your own.
8 'stalked off' What other ways of walking are there?

Write Now

1 Write a story called 'The Great Bike Race'.
2 Describe how you would feel towards the end of a match if your team was just leading.
3 Make a list of the different types of dogs.
4 'dogs look like their owners' Describe someone who might own a bulldog or a poodle.
5 Describe any silly race you had as a child.